CAMBRIDGE PET

PRACTICE TESTS

for the Preliminary English Test

Dorothy Adams

with Diane Flanel Piniaris

CENGAGE
Learning®

Australia • Brazil • Japan • Korea • Mexico • Singapore • Spain • United Kingdom • United States

Contents

Introduction

What makes this practice test book different from other test books available?

Cambridge PET Practice Tests is different because it is more than just a book of practice tests. It has been designed not only to familiarise students with the format and content of each part of the examination, but it also provides them with ample practice and a chance to improve the skills they need to do well.

The book contains:

- 6 complete practice tests
- An in-depth look and an exam technique section for each paper (see Test One)
- Hints on how to approach each exercise type
- Thorough guidance on Writing tasks, supported by model answers and paragraph plans in the Teacher's Book
- Extensive Speaking preparation designed to build confidence and reduce anxiety by providing helpful strategies for each part of the exam
- 'Test Your Vocabulary' exercises that recycle vocabulary encountered in each test

The 6 tests may be assigned for homework or done in class under timed conditions.

Cambridge Preliminary English Test (PET): A brief outline of each paper

PAPER 1: READING AND WRITING (1 hour 30 minutes)

- **Reading 5 parts (35 items)**

  Part 1 – **Multiple-choice (3 options):** 5 items focusing on the gist of 5 short real-life texts (e.g., signs, notes, labels)

  Part 2 – **Matching:** 5 descriptions of people to be matched to 8 short adapted/authentic texts

  Part 3 – **True-false:** 10 items testing understanding of a factual text (e.g., brochure or website)

  Part 4 – **Multiple-choice (4 options):** 5 items testing global meaning, attitude, opinion and writer's purpose in a longer text

  Part 5 – **Multiple-choice cloze (4 options):** 10 items focusing on use of vocabulary and grammatical patterns in a factual or narrative text.

- **Writing 3 parts**

  Part 1 – **Sentence transformations:** 5 theme-related items testing grammar and ability to rephrase. Students are given a sentence, then asked to fill in 1–3 missing words in a gapped sentence of similar meaning.

  Part 2 – **Short message:** task (35–45 words) focusing on conveying specific ideas

  Part 3 – **Choice of story or informal letter:** longer piece of continuous writing (100 words) testing control, organization and range of language

PAPER 2: LISTENING (about 30 minutes)

- **4 parts (25 items)**

  Part 1 – **Multiple-choice (3 picture options):** 7 items based on identifying key information in short monologues or dialogues. Students choose the picture that best answers the narrator's question.

  Part 2 – **Multiple-choice (3 text options):** 6 items based on understanding specific information and detailed meaning in a long monologue or interview.

  Part 3 – **Gap-fill:** 6 items based on identifying and interpreting information in a longer monologue. Candidates fill in missing words/phrases in a page of notes summing up the monologue.

  Part 4 – **True-false:** 6 items focusing on comprehension of the speakers' attitudes and opinions in an informal dialogue.

Students hear each recording twice.

PAPER 3: SPEAKING (about 12 minutes)

Students are usually interviewed in pairs. Two examiners are present: one (the 'interlocutor') conducts the interview and assesses the candidates' overall performance, while the other (the 'assessor') evaluates discourse management and other criteria (see page 7) and does not take part in the conversation.

- **4 parts**   **Part 1 – Short questions:** Candidates respond to factual, personal questions from the examiner.

   Part 2 – Simulated situation: Candidates discuss a situation set up by the examiner. A picture sheet is provided to aid the interaction.

   Part 3 – Extended turn: Each candidate describes a photograph based on a common theme.

   Part 4 – General conversation: The candidates have a discussion about their preferences, opinions, experiences, etc. based on the theme in Part 3.

Marking system

Each section (Reading, Writing, Listening and Speaking) counts for 25% of the final mark.

There is no individual pass mark for each paper.

Passing grades are **Pass** (about 70%) and **Pass with merit** (about 85%). Failing grades are **Narrow fail** (within 5% of the pass mark) and **Fail**.

Each candidate receives a Statement of Results, which reports performance in each component as 'Exceptional', 'Good', 'Borderline' or 'Weak'.

For detailed information on how the Writing and Speaking sections are marked, see pages 6 and 7.

On the day of the PET examination

The PET exam is usually administered on fixed dates in March, May, June, November and December. Consult your local Cambridge ESOL representative for precise details.

The written parts of the examination normally take place in the morning. The Speaking test is often administered in the afternoon on the same day.

The papers are in the following order.

   Paper 1:   Reading and Writing
   Paper 2:   Listening
   Paper 3:   Speaking

There is a short break between Paper 1 and Paper 2. There is also a break between the Listening paper and the first scheduled Speaking test. Details of the time and date of the Speaking test will be stated on the form each candidate receives from the local test administration centre.

Candidates should bring the following items with them to the examination centre:

- Statement of Entry/Timetable
- legal identification, such as ID card or a current passport
- pencils
- a pencil sharpener
- an eraser

Assessment criteria for Paper 1: Writing, Parts 2 and 3

The tasks in Writing, Parts 2 and 3 are assessed according to different mark schemes, reflecting differences in the nature of the tasks.

Writing, Part 2 – Question 6 (Short Message)

This question is rated out of 5 marks. Answers are assessed according to the following mark scheme in conjunction with a task specific mark scheme listing the 3 elements that should be present in the answer.

Points	Criteria
5	All content elements covered appropriately. Message clearly communicated to reader.
4	All content elements adequately dealt with. Message communicated successfully, on the whole.
3	All content elements attempted. Message requires some effort by the reader; or 1 content element omitted but others clearly communicated.
2	2 content elements omitted, or unsuccessfully dealt with. Message only partly communicated to reader; or script may be slightly short (20-25 words).
1	Little relevant content and/or message requires excessive effort by the reader, or short (10-19 words).
0	Totally irrelevant or totally incomprehensible or too short (under 10 words).

Assessment of Writing, Part 3: Questions 7 and 8 (informal letter or story)

Part 3 offers a choice of task: either an informal letter or a story. Marks for this part are given according to the mark scheme below. The band score is translated to a mark out of 15.

Band	Criteria
5 **Very good attempt** Requires no effort by the reader	• Confident and ambitious use of language • Wide range of structures and vocabulary within the task set • Well organised and coherent through use of simple linking devices • Errors are minor and non-impeding
4 **Good attempt** Requires only a little effort by the reader	• Fairly ambitious use of language • More than adequate range of structures and vocabulary within the task set • Evidence of organisation and some linking of sentences • Some errors, generally non-impeding
3 **Adequate attempt** Requires some effort by the reader	• Language is unambitious, or if ambitious, flawed • Adequate range of structures and vocabulary • Some attempt at organisation; linking of sentences not always maintained • A number of errors may be present, but are mostly non-impeding
2 **Inadequate attempt** Requires considerable effort by the reader	• Language is simplistic/limited/repetitive • Inadequate range of structures and vocabulary • Some incoherence; erratic punctuation • Numerous errors, which sometimes impede communication
1 **Poor attempt** Requires excessive effort by the reader	• Severely restricted command of language • No evidence of range of structures and vocabulary • Seriously incoherent; absence of punctuation • Very poor control; difficult to understand
0 **Achieves nothing**	• Language impossible to understand, or totally irrelevant to task.

Assessment criteria for Paper 3: Speaking

General principles of assessment

- Candidates are assessed on their own individual performance and not in relation to each other.

- Candidates are assessed on their language skills, and not on their personality, intelligence or knowledge of the world.

- Candidates must be prepared to develop the conversation, where appropriate, and respond to set tasks.

- Prepared speeches are not acceptable.

The Speaking test carries a total of 25 marks and represents 25% of the total score. Both examiners assess the candidates according to set criteria. The interlocutor (i.e., the examiner who conducts the interview) awards up to 5 marks for global achievement, while the assessor awards up to 5 marks in each of the following areas: grammar and vocabulary; discourse management; pronunciation; and interactive communication.

Here is a summary of what is assessed in each category.

AREA	WHAT IS ASSESSED
Global achievement (overall performance)	The candidate's overall effectiveness in dealing with each of the 4 tasks (from the perspective of the interlocutor)
Grammar and vocabulary	The overall effectiveness of the grammatical structures and vocabulary that the candidate uses in dealing with the tasks, including: • accuracy • appropriate use • range
Discourse management	The coherence, extent and relevance of the candidate's individual contribution, including: • ability to maintain a coherent flow of language within a single utterance or over a string of utterances • relevance of response to what has gone before
Pronunciation	The overall impact of the candidate's pronunciation and the degree of effort required to understand the candidate, including • stress • rhythm • intonation • individual sounds
Interactive communication	The candidate's ability to use language to achieve meaningful communication, including: • initiating and responding without undue hesitation • using interactive strategies to maintain or repair communication • displaying sensitivity to the norms of turn-taking

An in-depth look

You have 1 hour and 30 minutes to complete Paper 1: Reading and Writing.

The Reading section has 5 parts.

PART 1   Questions 1–5 test your ability to understand short texts, such as signs and notices. Each text is followed by 3 options (A, B and C). You must chose the correct statement.

PART 2   Questions 6–10 test your understanding of factual material. The exercise consists of descriptions of 5 people and 8 short texts (e.g., books to buy). To do well, you must identify key points about each person and then read the short texts carefully to find similar information.

PART 3   Questions 11–20 test your understanding of a longer, factual text (e.g., a travel brochure). You are given 10 statements and must decide whether each is true or false. To do well, you must be able to scan the longer text to check the information in each statement.

PART 4   Questions 21–25 test your ability to understand the writer's purpose, the overall meaning of a text, and the writer's attitudes and opinions. There are 5 multiple-choice questions with 4 options (A, B, C and D).

PART 5   Questions 26–35 test your knowledge of grammar and vocabulary. The exercise consists of a short text with 10 gaps. You must complete each gap by choosing the correct word from 4 options (A, B, C and D).

The Writing section has 3 parts.

PART 1   Questions 1–5 test your knowledge of grammar. You are given a sentence and are asked to complete a second sentence so that it has the same meaning. You may fill in 1, 2 or 3 words.

PART 2   Question 6 tests your ability to write clear, accurate English. You must write a short message of 35 to 45 words. Your answer must include the 3 points in the question.

PART 3   Questions 7 and 8 test the range, clarity and accuracy of your written English. You must choose either Question 7 or Question 8, and write a **story** or **informal letter** of about 100 words. To do well, you must write a well-organised letter or story and use a range of grammar structures and vocabulary.

Marking scheme and answer sheet

- **The Reading section** is worth 35 marks. Each question is worth 1 mark. The section counts for 25% of your final mark.

- **The Writing section** is worth 25 marks. Questions 1–5 are worth 1 mark each; Question 6, 5 marks; and Question 7 or 8, 15 marks. The Writing section counts for 25% of your final mark.

You must write your answers in pencil on the separate answer sheet. You will <u>not</u> be given any extra time at the end to transfer your answers onto the answer sheet.

Remember: For Part 3 of the Writing section, you must write the number 7 or 8 in the box at the top of your answer sheet so the examiners know which question you are answering.

Exam technique

Manage your time carefully

- You have 1 hour and 30 minutes for the Reading and Writing Paper. This means that it's important to manage your time carefully. If you don't, you won't have enough time to do the Writing tasks.

- Here are some guidelines:

Reading (about 45 minutes)		Writing (about 45 minutes)	
Part 1	5 minutes	Part 1	5 minutes
Part 2	10 minutes	Part 2	10 minutes
Part 3	13 minutes	Part 3	30 minutes
Part 4	10 minutes		
Part 5	7 minutes		

Don't spend too much time on any one question

- Each question in Parts 1–5 of Reading and Part 1 of Writing is worth only 1 mark, so try not to spend too much time on any one question.

- If you're not sure of an answer, guess … and move on! You don't lose marks for wrong answers, and you have a good chance of gaining a mark if you guess correctly.

Leave time to plan, write and check your Writing tasks

- 40 minutes may seem like a long time for Parts 2 and 3 of the Writing section, but remember that you'll need time to **plan**, **write** and **check** your work.

- Remember that accurate spelling and grammar are very important here, so leave yourself enough time to read over your work.

Find your own rhythm

- These timings are only a rough guide.

- As you do the practice tests in this book, keep a record of your times and find a formula that works for you.

Reading

Part 1

Questions 1 – 5

Look at the text in each question.
What does it say?
Mark the correct letter **A**, **B** or **C** on your answer sheet.

Example:

0

A   Do not take photographs when speeding on this road.

B   Cameras are used to check your speed on this road.

C   You may use your high-speed camera on this road.

Answer:

1

Music in the Park
Tickets for Sunday's performance
SOLD OUT

A   No ticket is needed if you want to go to the performance on Sunday.

B   There are no more tickets left for the performance on Sunday.

C   Sunday's concert is cancelled because no tickets have been sold.

2

A   Eat 2 meals a day.

B   Take 2 tablets every day.

C   Eat before taking these tablets.

Hints on answering Reading, Part 1

- Read carefully, and think about the text: e.g., *Where would it appear? What is its purpose? Are there any visual clues that help me?*

- Think about the *general* meaning. Don't panic if you don't know every word.

- Don't choose an answer just because it contains some of the words in the text. The right answer will often rephrase the text using different words.

- Never leave an answer blank. If you're not sure of the answer, guess!

3

A There are 2 ways of crossing the road.

B Check for cars before crossing the road.

C You can cross the road in 2 places.

4

A The photographs in this envelope do not bend.

B Do not bend when you are taking photographs.

C Do not bend this envelope; it contains photographs.

5

A Phone Mary when you get home.

B Mary is arranging a meeting tonight.

C Mary will call when she gets back.

Part 2

Questions 6 – 10

The people below all want to buy books.
On the opposite page there are descriptions of 8 books.
Decide which book would be the most suitable for the following people.
For questions **6 – 10**, mark the correct letter (**A – H**) on your answer sheet.

---

6  Gwen's 2 grandsons like watching TV programmes about how to make things. Gwen doesn't want to spend a lot of money on arts and crafts. Neither boy has started school yet, so she'd like to buy a book with simple projects. ....

7  Christine is a working mother with 3 children (ages 5, 8 and 10), a husband and a dog. She does a lot of serious reading at work, so in her spare time she enjoys reading humorous books about families like her own. ....

8  Mark is a musician who enjoys reading books about the lives of popular TV personalities. He didn't like going to school very much, so he especially likes reading about famous people who also disliked school. ....

9  Alan is a football fanatic so he is looking for a book about the sport. He is also interested in fashion. Alan is married and has 2 young children. He doesn't like reading about people who have had difficult lives. ....

10  Paul loves reading magazines and books about 20th-century superstars. He also spends a lot of time looking at photographs of famous people and is very fond of all types of music. ....

Recommended New Books

A   **Amazing *Art Attack* Stuff**
Following the successful TV series, here's a special edition of the very best of *Art Attack* ideas for kids from 4 to 104! Neil Buchanan crams in over 80 of the most amazing art projects you can imagine, using things you can easily find in your home. All are easy to make, look cool and really work. This book proves that anyone can be a great artist!

B   **Make Your Own Finger Puppets**
This book shows you how to create finger puppets of your favourite animals. Just follow the step-by-step instructions, and there's a whole zoo waiting to be made: from frogs and dogs to lions and pandas. Why not make yourself a puppet theatre and perform a puppet play with your friends? Great for young actors and actresses. Age 5 and up.

C   **The Mummy Diary**
Linda Jones has been making readers laugh for several years now. In between writing book reviews and fashion columns for the local newspaper and teaching chemistry and mathematics at the local high school, she always finds time to spend quality time with her family. The description of the dog's birthday party is simply brilliant.

D   **A Mother's Love**
Difficult choices lie ahead for Eve and Eddie, long-time owners of the George Pub in Liverpool. Their life has never been easy but it hasn't been bad either, and they've always managed to feed and clothe their 3 daughters. Suddenly, a tragic event changes everything. *A Mother's Love* will break your heart – but it does have a happy ending.

E   **Sinatra**
The perfect gift for every Sinatra fan, this new biography tells the true story of the 20th century's greatest singer. From his childhood in New Jersey to his rise to fame, the book tells the story of Sinatra's life away from the studio and off screen. Containing over 700 photographs, many of which have never been seen before, this is the remarkable story of the wonderful man whose songs are loved by people of all ages.

F   **So Me**
TV presenter Graham Norton shows us what he is really like in this honest and very funny book. Follow Graham as he moves through life: from being dragged to school by his mother to being dragged to Sharon Stone's New Year's Eve party, and from sharing a small flat in London to buying Claudia Schiffer's townhouse in Manhattan. An amusing and sometimes moving account of a very interesting life.

G   **Gazza**
Paul Gascoine's book about life on and off the football pitch is the most amazing soccer story you'll ever read. Paul ('Gazza', to his fans) tells all about his injury in the World Cup Final and what really happened when he was dropped from the team. He also reveals new facts about his battle with alcohol.

H   **David Beckham: My Side**
Football genius, fashion trendsetter, loving husband and adoring father – no wonder David Beckham is so popular. We have read so much about him in magazines and newspapers that we know everything about him. Or do we? Read his book and discover the real David Beckham, superstar and dad.

Part 3

Questions 11 – 20

Look at the sentences below about a Scottish travel agent's Hollywood Heroes Tours.
Read the text on the opposite page to decide if each sentence is correct or incorrect.
If it is correct, mark **A** on your answer sheet.
If it is not correct, mark **B** on your answer sheet.

		A	B
11	Hollywood film-makers often go on these tours.	▭	▭
12	*Local Hero* was a film starring 2 famous actors.	▭	▭
13	Not all of the scenes from *Local Hero* were filmed in Morar and Pennan.	▭	▭
14	The actor David Niven was born in Scotland.	▭	▭
15	One of the tours visits places which were used in more than one film.	▭	▭
16	Some of the places on the Hollywood Heroes tour can only be reached on foot.	▭	▭
17	The company will supply special seats for young children.	▭	▭
18	You will have to buy your own lunch if you go on a full-day tour.	▭	▭
19	If you live in London, you can fly, drive or travel by train to Scotland.	▭	▭
20	If you want to be met at the airport, you will have to pay extra.	▭	▭

Explore Scotland on a Hollywood Heroes Tour

Hollywood film producers have the whole world to pick from, but they've often chosen to shoot their films in Scotland. Why? Take one of our popular Hollywood Heroes Tours and find out!

THE TOURS

- **Morar and Pennan**, where cinema stars Dustin Hoffman and Burt Lancaster filmed most of their scenes for *Local Hero*.
- **Killin and the Falls of Dochard**, where the footage of English actor David Niven driving past a waterfall in *Casino Royale* was shot.
- **The Isle of Skye**, where many of the scenes for *Flash Gordon* were shot.
- **St Andrews and Edinburgh**, where *Chariots of Fire*, with award-winning music by Greek composer Vangelis, was shot.
- **Glenfinnian and Glen Coe**, where Mel Gibson made his historical film *Braveheart*. This beautiful countryside was also the background for the Quidditch scenes in *Harry Potter and the Philosopher's Stone*.

The Isle of Skye

DETAILS

All tours are available between May and October. Tours are in chauffeur-driven vehicles. Some walking is required to reach most locations, and some locations do require quite a lot of walking. See our website for details.

Cost
£175 per day for up to 4 passengers, including full guide service. When you book, let us know the ages of children travelling with you so we can provide child car seats and/or booster seats.

Where you will stay
All accommodation is in 3- or 4-star hotels and is on a full-board basis*.

*Some tours are full-day tours, which means we will not return to the hotel for lunch. On these tours our clients can chose: a packed lunch provided by the hotel or meal vouchers, which can be exchanged for meals at selected local restaurants.

Travelling to Scotland
Most international airlines have scheduled flights to Scottish airports. There are also domestic flights from London and Manchester to Glasgow, Aberdeen and Edinburgh airports as well as excellent road and rail links. Your chauffeur will pick you up from any Scottish airport – there is no additional charge for airport transfers.

How to book
Visit our website for details of how to book this month's featured tour, or call freephone (0800) 123456. You can also order our brochure with details of these and other tours by filling in an online request form or by calling freephone (0800) 123457.

Part 4

Questions 21 – 25

Read the text and questions below.
For each question, mark the correct letter **A**, **B**, **C** or **D** on your answer sheet.

The Scorpion Family

When my son Martin brought home his new pet, I wasn't exactly thrilled. 'How awful,' I hear you say, but don't judge me yet – it was an emperor scorpion! Martin told me that the emperor scorpion is one of the most popular scorpions that are kept as pets. 'They look big and frightening,' he said, 'but they're not particularly dangerous to humans as their sting is quite harmless.' Well, it looked pretty dangerous to me!

Sam has escaped from his tank a few times, and I'll never forget the first time he did. We looked for him all over the house. Finally, I shone a torch behind the sofa and I saw something bright green. I didn't know it at the time, but when you shine a light on emperor scorpions, they become bright green. I thought it was one of my youngest son's toys. Imagine my horror when I picked it up!

Last year we bought Sam a partner called Samantha, and we are now the proud parents of an entire scorpion family. You should see the way Samantha carries her babies on her back. I am always afraid that she will drop them and they'll be injured, but she hasn't so far.

21   In this text, the writer is describing

    A   her son's emperor scorpions.

    B   the most popular family pets.

    C   why scorpions are dangerous.

    D   how to take care of scorpions.

22   What does the writer say about emperor scorpions?

    A   They are expensive to feed.

    B   They are popular pets.

    C   They are very frightening.

    D   They have a dangerous sting.

23   The first time the writer had to look for Sam, she

   A   found him hiding behind a green toy on the sofa.

   B   knew he would turn green if she shone a torch on him.

   C   picked the scorpion up, not realising what it was.

   D   searched for a long time without any success.

24   What does the writer say about the baby scorpions?

   A   Their mother used to carry them on her back.

   B   Their mother seemed afraid that she would drop them.

   C   They were afraid of falling off their mother's back.

   D   They made her feel very proud of her own family.

25   What might the writer say about her son's pet?

   A
   > I wish my son would sell his family of emperor scorpions.

   B
   > I didn't like my son's choice of pet at first, but I do now.

   C
   > Emperor scorpions are dangerous and should not be bought as pets.

   D
   > My son's pets are awful, and they keep climbing out of their tanks.

Part 5

Questions 26 – 35

Read the text below and choose the correct word for each space.
For each question, mark the correct letter **A**, **B**, **C** or **D** on your answer sheet.

Example:

| 0 | **A** largest | **B** huge | **C** big | **D** greater |

Answer:

| 0 | A | B | C | D |

The Country's Biggest Art Gallery

Tendale Stadium is about to become the country's **(0)** .... art gallery. Local youngsters are invited to join special **(26)** .... workshops which will be run **(27)** .... a group of **(28)** .... famous artists. Each of **(29)** .... will produce an autographed piece of art, which will be **(30)** .... on the stadium walls for everyone to see.

The project is expected to last until the **(31)** .... of the year, and participants will get to fill the stadium walls with huge pictures of their **(32)** .... sporting, acting, and singing heroes.

Tuition, paints and equipment will be provided free **(33)** .... charge, so participants don't need to bring **(34)** .... – except, of course, **(35)** .... !

26	**A** painting	**B** paint	**C** painted	**D** paint's
27	**A** from	**B** for	**C** by	**D** of
28	**A** too	**B** very	**C** enough	**D** so
29	**A** we	**B** them	**C** they	**D** us
30	**A** displayed	**B** appeared	**C** decorated	**D** reviewed
31	**A** end	**B** finish	**C** conclusion	**D** last
32	**A** famous	**B** best	**C** popular	**D** favourite
33	**A** to	**B** for	**C** of	**D** from
34	**A** somebody	**B** nothing	**C** anything	**D** anyone
35	**A** himself	**B** herself	**C** itself	**D** themselves

Writing

Part 1

Questions 1 – 5

Here are some sentences about families.
For each question, complete the second sentence so that it means the same as the first.
Use no more than 3 words.
Write only the missing words on your answer sheet.
You may use this page for any rough work.

Example:

0   My brother should get his car washed.

      My brother's car …………............………..……. **washing**.

Answer:	**0**	*needs*

---

1   My sister doesn't like ice cream as much as I do.

      I like ice cream …………...........………..…. **my sister does**.

2   My parents think I should apply to university next year.

      My parents would like …………...........………..…. **apply to university next year**.

3   The last time we saw our cousins was a month ago.

      We …………...........………..…. **seen our cousins for a month**.

4   I can't go to the party if I don't do my homework.

      I can't go to the party unless …………...........………..…. **my homework**.

5   The woman you were speaking to is my aunt.

      The woman to …………...........………..…. **were speaking is my aunt**.

Hints on answering Writing, Part 1

This part tests your ability to express the same idea in 2 ways. The example below tests the different verb tenses used with *for* and *ago*.

I haven't seen Mary for several years.

The last time I ....saw Mary............. **was several years ago**.

Technique

Always try to work out what grammar is being tested.

- Think about both sentences: e.g., Do they express past, present or future time? Are they suggestions, offers or requests? Do they express possibility, advice or necessity?

- What similarities and differences do you notice?

- What is missing in the second sentence: e.g., verb? subject + verb? verb + object? verb + adverb?

- Check your answer. Make sure:
  (a)   You have not repeated any of the words before or after the gap.
  (b)   Your new sentence means *exactly* the same as the original.

Remember

- You can only fill in 1, 2 or 3 words in each gap.

- Contractions like *don't*, *can't*, and *won't* are counted as 2 words; *cannot* is 1 word.

- You will lose marks for incorrect spelling, so check your answers carefully.

Part 2

Question 6

You are on holiday with your family.

Write a postcard to an English friend of yours. In your postcard, you should:

- say where you are on holiday.

- write about some of the things you have done.

- arrange to meet your friend when you get back.

Write **35 – 45 words** on your answer sheet.

Part 3

Write an answer to **one** of the questions (**7** or **8**) in this part.
Write your answer in about **100 words** on your answer sheet.
Put the question number in the box at the top of your answer sheet.

Question 7

• Your English teacher has asked you to write a story.

• Your story must have the following title:

     A really strange family

• Write your **story** on your answer sheet.

Question 8

• This is part of a letter you receive from your English friend, Sheila.

> I have just joined a new evening class to learn how to paint!
> It's fantastic. The other students are really friendly.
> Do you have any hobbies?

• Now write a letter to Sheila, telling her about your hobbies.

• Write your **letter** on your answer sheet.

Hints on writing the story in Writing, Part 3

Part 3 gives you a choice of tasks: you may choose to write a **story** or an **informal letter** of about 100 words. If you choose the story, you will be given either a short title or the first sentence. You may not change the title or sentence in any way. Before you begin, read the instructions carefully. Then follow these steps:

Think
- What kind of story will it be: funny, frightening, happy, sad?
- Who or what is the story about? Where does it take place?

Plan
- Organise your story into paragraphs.
- Write down a few ideas for each paragraph, so you don't forget your ideas.
- Use this simple formula to help you.

Beginning	In the first paragraph, say what was happening as the story begins. This sets the scene and lets you introduce people and places.
Middle	Tell the middle of the story (1–2 paragraphs).
Ending	Say how the story ends.

Write
- Use your paragraph plan to write your story.
- Include adjectives and adverbs to describe people, places and events.
- Connect your ideas with linking words and time expressions to help guide your reader through the story. Use expressions like *first*, *then*, *next*, *later*, *the next day* and *finally*.

Check
- Reread your work and check your grammar and spelling carefully.
- Make sure you have not written too many or too few words.

An in-depth look

The Listening paper takes about 30 minutes, plus 6 minutes at the end to transfer your answers onto the answer sheet. The paper has 4 parts. <u>You will hear each part twice.</u>

PART 1   Questions 1–7 test your ability to listen for key information. Each item you hear contains a question and a short dialogue or monologue taken from everyday life (e.g., a conversation between friends or a monologue such as part of a news broadcast or announcement). In your test booklet, you will see the question and 3 pictures. As you listen, you must choose the picture (**A**, **B** or **C**) that best answers the question.

PART 2   Questions 8–13 test your ability to listen for specific information and understand the detailed meaning of a longer text (either a monologue or an interview). In your test booklet, you will see 6 multiple-choice items in the form of a question or statement with 3 possible options. As you listen, you must choose the option (**A**, **B** or **C**) that answers the question or completes the statement.

PART 3   Questions 14–19 test your ability to identify, understand and interpret information in an extended text. In your test booklet, you will see a page of notes that summarise the information you hear. The notes contain 6 numbered gaps that you must fill with words you hear. Incorrect spelling is acceptable, except for high-frequency words or words which are spelt out in the recording.

PART 4   Questions 20–25 test your ability to understand a speaker's attitude or opinion as you listen to a dialogue (usually between a man and a woman). In your test booklet, you will see 6 statements. You must decide whether the statements are true or false, according to what you hear.

Marking scheme

There are 25 questions in the Listening paper. Each question is worth 1 mark.

The Listening paper counts for 25% of your final mark.

Exam technique

During the test

- Look at the questions *before* you listen. This will help you decide what you need to listen for.

- Don't worry if you hear any unfamiliar words. If you focus on the *general* meaning of what you hear, you will still be able to answer most of the questions.

- Answer as many questions as you can the first time you listen to the recording.

- Use the second time to check your answers and complete anything you missed the first time.

- Answer *all* the questions. You won't lose marks for wrong answers, so if you don't know the answer, guess!

At the end of the test

- You have 6 minutes to transfer your answers from your test booklet onto the special answer sheet.

- As you transfer each answer, check that you have placed it next to the correct question number on your answer sheet.

Part 1

Questions 1 – 7

There are 7 questions in this part.
For each question, there are 3 pictures and a short recording.
Choose the correct picture and put a tick (✔) in the box below it.

Example:

0 What time are they meeting?

  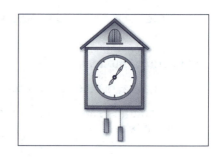

A ☐   B ✔   C ☐

---

1 What does the woman buy?

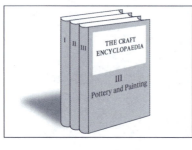  

A ☐   B ☐   C ☐

2 Where did the man put the suntan cream?

  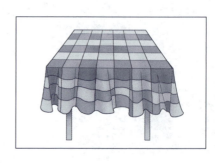

A ☐   B ☐   C ☐

Hints on answering Listening, Part 1

Before you listen

- Read the question carefully.
- Notice the first word (or phrase): e.g., *who, what, which, when, where, how, how often*.
- Study the pictures: What do they show? How are they similar? How are they different?

The first time you listen

- Pay attention to clues that relate to the first word (or phrase) in each question.
- Don't answer until the conversation finishes. The answer may be at the very end.
- Answer as many questions as possible.

The second time you listen

- Check your answers to the questions you've already filled in.
- Listen carefully for answers to the questions you did not answer.
- If you're still not sure, guess! You have nothing to lose.

---

3 How many of her friends are coming from London?

A ☐   B ☐   C ☐

4 Which TV programme does he ask his mother to record?

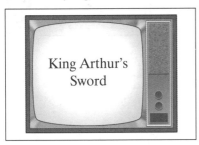  

A ☐   B ☐   C ☐

5 Where does the woman tell the man to meet her?

A ☐

B ☐

C ☐

6 What did the woman forget to buy?

A ☐

B ☐

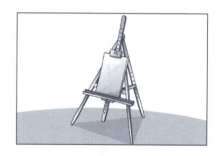

C ☐

7 Which beach is she talking about?

A ☐

B ☐

C ☐

Part 2

Questions 8 – 13

You will hear someone reading the news on a local radio programme.
For each question, put a tick (✔) in the correct box.

---

8 Harry Bolton

A was a lifeguard for a year. ☐

B works as a lifeguard now. ☐

C used to be a lifeguard. ☐

9 When can you phone the craft centre about courses?

A from 9–10 am every weekday ☐

B from 7–9.30 every evening ☐

C from 9–12 am every Saturday ☐

10 Where can you get free rubber gloves for Clean Beach Day?

A from the reception desk at the radio station ☐

B from the local newspaper office ☐

C from any supermarket ☐

11 The new film is on at the Film Centre

A at 7 and 9 every day till next Friday. ☐

B at midnight on Saturday. ☐

C on Friday only. ☐

12 The radio programme *Cinema* is

A about all kinds of films. ☐

B a quiz show. ☐

C about films with superheroes. ☐

13 The person in the show on Sunday evening is

A a teacher. ☐

B a sports instructor. ☐

C a football player. ☐

Part 3

Questions 14 – 19

You will hear a teacher talking about courses at a craft centre.
For each question, fill in the missing information in the numbered space.

GRANGE CRAFT CENTRE

Courses available

- 30-week painting course
- 30-week **(14)** ………………......................… course
- 30-week drawing course
- **(15)** ………………......................… -week sculpture course

Course days

- Pottery and drawing: Mondays and **(16)** ………………......................…
- Painting and sculpture: on Tuesdays and Thursdays

NOTE: All students will have to be at the centre at weekends at the end of the year to help teachers set up end-of-year exhibitions.

Course levels

There are 3 course levels: beginners, intermediate and advanced.
Students who wish to join the intermediate class must have completed the
(17) ………………......................… class, and those who wish to join the advanced
class must have completed the beginners class and the intermediate class∗.

∗We also accept students who have completed these courses at the Salton Craft Centre.

Class times

- Beginners: **(18)** ………………......................…
- Intermediate: 5 – 6 pm
- Advanced: 8 – 9 pm

Enrolment

Enrolment forms must be returned by the end of the **(19)** ………………......................… .

Part 4

Questions 20 – 25

Look at the 6 sentences for this part.
You will hear a conversation between a woman, Kate, and her friend, Alan, about going to the beach.
Decide if each sentence is correct or incorrect.
If it is correct, put a tick (✔) in the box under **A** for **YES**. If it is not correct, put a tick (✔) in the box under **B** for **NO**.

		A YES	B NO
20	Kate thinks that Sandy Bay will be too crowded.	☐	☐
21	Alan wants to go to the beach with Kevin.	☐	☐
22	Kate doesn't think the snack bar will have good food.	☐	☐
23	Alan thinks it's a good idea to bring their own food.	☐	☐
24	Kate insists on buying food from the supermarket.	☐	☐
25	Alan thinks there will be a lot of traffic in town.	☐	☐

An in-depth look

Paper 3: Speaking lasts for 10 to 12 minutes. Usually, 2 candidates are examined by 2 examiners; if you are in the last session, you may be 1 of 3 candidates. During the exam, 1 of the examiners ('the interlocutor') speaks to the candidates and explains the tasks, while the other examiner ('the assessor') listens. At the end, both examiners assess your performance.

The Speaking paper has 4 parts. Each part lasts about 3 minutes.

PART 1   tests your ability to give information about yourself (for example, where you live, your interests, your studies). Both candidates have a short conversation with the examiner.

PART 2   tests your ability to interact in English by making and responding to suggestions, discussing alternatives and agreeing or disagreeing. You are given a picture sheet with some ideas for you to discuss with the other candidate.

PART 3   tests your ability to describe. You will be given a photograph and asked to spend about a minute describing it. Your photograph and the other candidate's photograph will have the same 'theme': for example, 'work' or 'leisure activities'.

PART 4   tests your ability to have a discussion with your partner about your opinions, likes/dislikes, preferences and experiences. You will be asked to talk about a topic related to the theme in Part 3.

Marking scheme

The Speaking paper is worth 25 points. It counts for 25% of your final mark.

You will be given a mark from 1 to 5 for each of the following categories:

* **Grammar and vocabulary:** your ability to use grammar and vocabulary accurately and appropriately

* **Discourse management:** your ability to keep the conversation flowing and to answer questions with well-developed responses (rather than single-word answers)

* **Pronunciation:** your ability to pronounce English words clearly enough to be understood

* **Interactive communication:** your ability to communicate with both the examiner and the other candidate

* **Overall performance:** how well you have dealt with all of the tasks

Exam technique

Before the exam

It is natural for candidates to be nervous before the PET Speaking test. Here are some ideas to help you relax:

- Take several deep breaths before you go into the room.

- Look at the examiners and smile; it will help everyone feel more relaxed.

- Take a few seconds to get comfortable in your chair.

- Remember that the examiners are used to talking to candidates with trembling hands and shaky voices. They expect you to be nervous, and it's part of their job to help you feel more relaxed and comfortable.

When the exam begins

Here is what you can expect to hear from the lead examiner when you enter the room:

> **Examiner:** Good morning/afternoon/evening.
> Can I have your mark sheets, please?

Next, the examiner will introduce himself/herself and the second examiner.

> **Examiner:** I'm … [*says name*], and this is … [*introduces second examiner*]. He/She is just going to listen to us.

After that, the examiner will ask you and your partner your names. Be prepared to spell your surname using English letters (for example: 'Smith. That's S - M - I - T - H.')

Part 1 (2 – 3 minutes)

- Where do you live?

- Do you work or are you a student in ……..?

- Do you enjoy studying English? Why (not)?

- Do you think that English will be useful to you in the future?

- What do you enjoy doing in your free time?

Part 2 (2 – 3 minutes)

I'm going to describe a situation to you. You are planning to go to the beach with your friends this weekend. Talk together about the activities you can do at the beach and then decide which would be the best way of spending time at the beach .

If you turn to page 146, you'll find some ideas to help you.

> [Pause for 4 – 5 seconds]

I'll say that again. You are planning to go to the beach with your friends this weekend. Talk together about the activities you can do at the beach, and then decide which would be the best way of spending time at the beach.

All right? Now talk together.

Part 3 (3 minutes)

Now, I'd like each of you to talk on your own about something. I'm going to give each of you a photograph showing something you can do when you're on holiday.

Candidate A, please look at photograph A on page 147.

Candidate B, you can also look at **Candidate A**'s photo, but I'll give you your photograph in a moment.

Candidate A, please tell us what you can see in your photograph?

> [Allow about 1 minute.]

Candidate B, please look at photograph B on page 147. It also shows something you can do when you're on holiday.

Candidate A, you can look also look at **Candidate B**'s photograph.

Now, **Candidate B**, please tell us what you can see in the photograph.

> [Allow about 1 minute.]

Part 4 (3 minutes)

Your photographs in Part 3 showed things you can do when you are on holiday. Now, I'd like you to talk together about the things you liked to do on holiday when you were younger and the things you like to do now.

Hints on answering the examiner's questions in Speaking, Part 1

In this part of the Speaking test the examiner will ask you and your partner some questions on general topics such as where you live, your studies, and your hobbies and interests.

Here are some helpful tips:

- Listen carefully when the examiner is speaking.

- If you don't understand a question, ask the examiner to repeat it. (Remember to say 'please'; it always creates a good impression.)

- When you answer, try to give a reason or an example. For example: 'Yes, I enjoy studying English because my teacher is nice and the other students are very friendly.'

- Don't forget to look at the examiner when you speak. It will make you seem more confident.

Be yourself

- Answer each question honestly and naturally. For example, if you don't have any hobbies or you don't like any of the subjects you are studying at school, don't be afraid to say so. Remember that the examiners are marking you on how well you speak; they are not marking you on your hobbies or your opinions about school.

- Avoid preparing a speech. The examiners will recognise this and politely ask you to stop speaking before you have finished.

Be a good listener

- When it's your partner's turn to answer the questions in Part 1, relax and pay attention to what is being said. Look at your partner, nod when you agree, and laugh if he or she makes a joke. This makes a good impression on the examiners and may play a role in the mark they will give you for your overall performance.

Reading

Questions 1 – 5

Look at the text in each question.
What does it say?
Mark the correct letter **A**, **B** or **C** on your answer sheet.

Example:

0

A Do not take photographs when speeding on this road.

B Cameras are used to check your speed on this road.

C You may use your high-speed camera on this road.

Answer: 0   A   B   C

1

A Only groups of 18 children are allowed in the bar.

B This bar is too small for groups with 18 children.

C You must be at least 18 years old to go into the bar.

2

A It is safe to use the cream as many as 8 times a day.

B If you use the cream 8 times a day, the pain will go away.

C Use the cream within 8 days or the pain will not go away.

3

- Empty contents of pack into a heat-proof dish.
- Add 1/2 cup milk.
- Cook on high for 2 minutes.
- Allow to cool before serving.

A This food tastes better if it is served hot.

B You must add milk to this food before cooking.

C This food will be ready to eat in 2 minutes.

4

Saver tickets cannot be used at weekends

A It costs less to travel on Saturday and Sunday.

B You can only use Saver tickets during the week.

C You cannot buy Saver tickets at the weekend.

5

John,
Problems with cooker again. Oven light on - not heating food. Please call Gas Board.
Gina

A The person who prepares Gina's food is serving cold meals.

B Gina wants John to phone the Gas Board about her cooker.

C Gina's cooker does not work when she turns the light on.

Part 2

Questions 6 – 10

The people below all want to buy a mobile phone.
On the opposite page there are descriptions of 8 mobile phones.
Decide which mobile phone would be the most suitable for the following people.
For questions **6 – 10**, mark the correct letter (**A – H**) on your answer sheet.

---

6  As a reporter, Jason travels a lot, so he is looking for a mobile phone he can use all over the world. He also wants it to have a world map and a very long battery life. ....

7  George is a sailing enthusiast who needs a phone which is waterproof. He would also like it to take photos and record videos. ....

8  Alice is a pensioner. She finds it hard to use ordinary mobile phones because the numbers are too small to see. She also has trouble using them with her hearing aid. ....

9  Sue is a university student who doesn't have a lot of extra money. She wants a mobile phone with a camera and a radio in her favourite colour, blue. ....

10  Brenda wants a phone she can use in Europe and North America. She needs to know if calls are from friends and family or business contacts. She is now living in the USA. ....

Hints on answering Reading, Part 2

In this part, you must match 5 descriptions of people to 5 short texts from a total of 8. Always read the instructions carefully to find out what you need to match. Then follow these steps:

* Underline key information for each person. This is usually found after words such as *enjoy*, *like*, *love*, *need*, *want*, *interested in*, *fond of*.

* Circle negative verb phrases such as *doesn't like*, *dislikes*, *isn't fond of*. This helps you to focus on the person's dislikes as well as their likes.

* Quickly scan the texts to find the text that best matches each person.

Remember:

* The information in the text may not be expressed in exactly the same way as in the description.

* The text you select must meet *all* the key information in the description.

Hot Deals – Mobile Phones

A Use this quad band mobile phone all over the world. Longest battery life on the market. The special SatNav guidance system will bring maps of every country right to your screen. It also finds you places to eat at and transport information. Too good to be missed at £99.99.

B With a 3.5-inch full-colour screen, this phone has the biggest display on the market. It's also 'voice activated': all you need to do is tell it what you want it to do! Speaker phone function also included. Home delivery at no extra cost. Buy now for only £35.

C This handy 2-megapixel camera-phone comes with a lovely leather case to protect it from scratches. The 128-megabyte memory lets you take hundreds of photographs. A great deal at only £150.

D This great phone has a compact, slim design, lots of games and a built-in camera. Extras include radio headphones and interchangeable covers in red, blue, green and purple. A real bargain at £50.

E If you need a phone for Europe and the USA, this one's for you. Includes 'special ring tone' function that allows you to assign a special ring for up to 50 numbers, so you know who's on the line without looking. Connect it to your laptop to browse the Internet and receive e-mails. Free delivery worldwide. Special offer: £200.

F This 2-megabyte camera-phone and mp3 player is great for taking photographs and can store up to 45 minutes of music. As you'd expect, it comes with a huge range of extras including PC software and a 64-megabyte memory stick. Available in fashionable shades of red, blue or green. An excellent buy at only £145.

G This phone has a full-colour screen and lots of special features. As well as allowing you to record videos and take colour photographs, it even lets you record your voice. It comes with a special plastic cover, which means you never have to worry about getting it wet. Price: £260.

H If you travel around Europe, this phone could be what you're looking for. It is dual band, which means you can use it anywhere in Europe. It also has a very large address book, where you can store up to 500 phone numbers. The price: £180, with free delivery anywhere in Europe.

Part 3

Questions 11 – 20

Look at the sentences below about adventure activities at the Quest Centre in Wales.
Read the text on the opposite page to decide if each sentence is correct or incorrect.
If it is correct, mark **A** on your answer sheet.
If it is not correct, mark **B** on your answer sheet.

		A	B
11	You have to take a test before you can take part in the mountain biking event.	⬜	⬜
12	If you go mountain biking, you need to be prepared for bad weather.	⬜	⬜
13	You will use dangerous equipment if you sign up for the climbing activity.	⬜	⬜
14	The survival techniques course is only held on certain dates.	⬜	⬜
15	One of the instructors was killed while he was abseiling.	⬜	⬜
16	The abseiling and rope-climbing course is more expensive than the climbing course.	⬜	⬜
17	Adventure Weekends are only available until the end of August.	⬜	⬜
18	You need to bring food with you on an Adventure Weekend.	⬜	⬜
19	A group of 7 will pay less to take part in these activities.	⬜	⬜
20	You do not need to pay extra to hire special equipment.	⬜	⬜

The Quest Centre

Set in the wild Welsh countryside, the Quest Centre offers a wide range of activities for teenagers, from archery to rope climbing. Want to try something new? Why not take part in one of our special adventure activities?

MOUNTAIN BIKING

25th March - 8th April, 10 am - 6 pm

Want to put your mountain bike to the test? Join our guide for a ride on the wild side. Don't forget to bring waterproof clothes with you. Cost: £15 per rider.

CLIMBING

1st - 31st May, 10 am - 6 pm

Try out your mountain-climbing skills in the local countryside. Don't worry! We won't be doing anything dangerous: just short, safe climbs so you can get used to the equipment. Cost: £130 per person.

SURVIVAL TECHNIQUES

Daily, all year round, 10 am - 5 pm

Equip yourself with basic survival skills by taking part in this special 1-day course absolutely free of charge. Learn survival techniques like how to light a fire, build a shelter, find food and water, and cook over a campfire. Who knows? The life you may need to save some day could be your own.

ABSEILING AND ROPE CLIMBING

27th August, 10 am - 8 pm

If you've been dying to learn about abseiling and rope climbing, now is your chance! Ken Wallace, our professional coach, will teach you everything you need to know on this special 1-day course. Cost: £150 per person.

ADVENTURE WEEKENDS

Every Saturday and Sunday from 20th July - 31st August
10 am Saturday - 7 pm Sunday

A great opportunity to try out climbing, abseiling and rope climbing, plus other outdoor activities like archery, canoeing, horse riding. Cost: from £400 per person, including meals and accommodation.

Please note:

- Phone the number at the bottom of the page for an application form.
- All activities are suitable for beginners.
- 20% DISCOUNT for groups of 6 or more.
- Prices include the hire of any special equipment which may be necessary.

Dates/Hours of operation

25th March - 19th July: 10 am to 4 pm

20th July - 31st August: 10 am to 7.30 pm

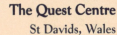

The Quest Centre
St Davids, Wales
Telephone: (0800) 34655

Part 4

Questions 21 – 25

Read the text and questions below.
For each question, mark the correct letter **A**, **B**, **C** or **D** on your answer sheet.

Christie Saunders, Signer

I was 20 years old, and my parents were looking forward to the day when I would be earning my own living. Unfortunately, I had absolutely no idea what I wanted my future occupation to be. The only thing I did know was that I did not want to spend the next 45 years teaching, being a nurse or sitting in an office.

But that was before the postman delivered a catalogue of courses that were being offered at the local college. As I looked through it, I was attracted by a page that talked about the difficulties faced by deaf people in their everyday lives and how students could help by learning sign language. It went on to say that graduates of the course usually find work in various organisations, such as law companies, the Stock Exchange, insurance companies and banks. Then I saw something that really caught my eye: 'Signers' are also needed for sporting events, concerts, theatrical performances and, believe it or not, circuses! By the time I got to the bottom of the page, I knew I had found the perfect occupation.

I enrolled on the course, which to my parents' great delight was free of charge. The course was brilliant. My favourite part was the final lesson, when our teacher asked us to sign our favourite song. It was really difficult because not only did we have to sign the words, but we also had to find a way of showing whether the song was happy or sad and whether the beat was slow or fast. It was the hardest thing I have ever done – but also the most rewarding.

21 What does Christie describe in the text?

    A   how she chose her career

    B   how she lives with deaf people

    C   how difficult sign language is to learn

    D   how deaf people learn sign language

22 Christie suggests that she

    A   could not find a job as a nurse or a teacher.

    B   has never liked being in a teacher's office.

    C   would not get a job until she was at least 45.

    D   didn't want to work in a school or hospital.

23   According to the catalogue Christie read, when students finish a sign language course, they

   A   do not have to work with deaf people.

   B   can work in a variety of different places.

   C   may not always find a job in their chosen field.

   D   almost always start their career in a law company.

24   The part of the course Christie enjoyed the most was when

   A   she realised that her parents didn't have to pay.

   B   her teacher sang a very sad song to the class.

   C   she had to sign a song for the last lesson.

   D   she had to sing a song with a fast beat.

25   Which of the following best describes Christie?

   A

a young deaf woman who wants to help the deaf

   B

a young woman who has found her ideal career

   C

a young woman who wants to be a businesswoman

   D

a young woman who wants to write songs for the deaf

Part 5

Questions 26 – 35

Read the text below and choose the correct word for each space.
For each question, mark the correct letter **A**, **B**, **C** or **D** on your answer sheet.

Example:

0	**A** disappointing	**B** embarrassed	**C** annoying	**D** saddening

Answer:

0	A	B	C	D
	—	—	▬	—

Barking Dogs Can Seriously Damage Your Health

We all know that barking dogs can be **(0)** ………. , but did you know that the sound **(26)** ……….
be loud enough to seriously harm your health? Scientists use a unit called a decibel to **(27)** ……….
sound levels, and experts agree that **(28)** ………. we listen to noises above 80 decibels for a long
time, it will damage our hearing.

When a dog barks **(29)** ………. , the sound level can be **(30)** ………. high as 110 decibels.
(31) ………. means it is louder than busy traffic (70 decibels), an alarm clock (80 decibels) and a
lawn mower (90 decibels), **(32)** ………. not quite as loud as a jet engine (120 decibels). In contrast,
normal conversation is only 60 decibels.

Dogs are not the **(33)** ………. animals, though. The call of the blue whale is a deafening
188 decibels, which can be **(34)** ………. for hundreds of miles. Luckily for you and me, they usually
make the sound **(35)** ………. water!

26	**A** could	**B** will	**C** must	**D** should

27	**A** lower	**B** measure	**C** count	**D** decrease

28	**A** while	**B** since	**C** unless	**D** if

29	**A** hard	**B** hardly	**C** loud	**D** loudly

30	**A** as	**B** too	**C** so	**D** enough

31	**A** They	**B** He	**C** This	**D** It

32	**A** so	**B** either	**C** or	**D** but

33	**A** friendliest	**B** noisiest	**C** softest	**D** largest

34	**A** heard	**B** listened	**C** seen	**D** made

35	**A** beyond	**B** on	**C** under	**D** down

Writing

Questions 1 – 5

Here are some sentences about a trip to a safari park.
For each question, complete the second sentence so that it means the same as the first.
Use no more than 3 words.
Write only the missing words on your answer sheet.
You may use this page for any rough work.

Example:

0   The lions are fed 3 times a day.

    They …………………………….….. **the lions 3 times a day**.

Answer:

0	*feed*

---

1   Watching wild animals is exciting.

    It's exciting …….…................……. **wild animals**.

2   It was Penny's first visit to a safari park.

    Penny had …….…............…………... **to a safari park before**.

3   It isn't necessary to bring food with you, as the park has many places to eat.

    The park has many places to eat, so you …….…....………………..…. **to bring your own food**.

4   Dave said the monkeys were more interesting than the elephants.

    Dave said the elephants were not …….……............…………. **the monkeys**.

5   We'd like to go back to the park because it was fantastic.

    The park was …….…...........……....……. **that we'd like to go back**.

Part 2

Question 6

You are thinking of applying to university.

Write an e-mail to a friend of yours. In your e-mail you should:

• say what subject you are thinking of studying.

• explain why you are interested in that subject.

• ask what your friend thinks about your choice of subject.

Write **35 – 45** words on your answer sheet.

Hints on answering Writing, Part 2

In Part 2 you must write a short message of 35 – 45 words.

Technique

There are always 3 points that you must include in your answer. (If you don't include 1 or more points, you will lose marks.) To make sure you include all 3, use the points in the question to make a chart like the one below. Then use the sentences in the last column in your answer.

SAY	which subject I am thinking of studying	*I'm thinking of studying ...*
EXPLAIN	**why I am interested in it**	*I'm really interested in ... because ...*
ASK	**my friend for his/her opinion.**	*Please write soon and tell me what you think about ...*

Remember

• You are writing to a friend, so the style should be informal and friendly. Use short forms like *I'm, I wasn't, you're, you weren't* where possible.

• Count your words and make sure you have stayed within the limit (35 to 45 words).

Part 3

Write an answer to **one** of the questions (**7** or **8**) in this part.
Write your answer in about **100 words** on your answer sheet.
Put the question number in the box at the top of your answer sheet.

Question 7

• This is part of a letter you receive from an English penfriend.

> I'm so excited! My parents just gave me a new mobile phone for my birthday – just the one I wanted!
>
> What's the best present you've ever received? Why did you like it so much?

• Now write a letter, answering your penfriend's questions.

• Write your **letter** on your answer sheet.

Question 8

• Your English teacher has asked you to write a story.

• Your story must have the following title:

   The day everything changed

• Write your **story** on your answer sheet.

Hints on writing the letter in Writing, Part 3

Part 3 gives you a choice of tasks: you may choose to write a **story** or an **informal letter** of about 100 words. If you choose the letter, you will be given a short extract from a letter from a friend. Read the instructions carefully. Then follow these steps.

Think

- Who do I have to I write to?
- What do I have to write about?

Plan

Beginning   In the first paragraph, thank your penfriend for his/her letter and say why you are writing.

Middle   Answer your penfriend's questions. Remember to support your answer with explanations and/or examples (1–2 paragraphs).

Ending   Ask your friend to write soon and say you are looking forward to hearing from him/her.

Write

- Use your paragraph plan to write your letter.
- Include adjectives and adverbs to describe people, places and events.
- Use linking words such as *so*, *because*, *and* or *but*.

Check

- Reread your work and check your grammar and spelling carefully.
- Make sure you have not written too many or too few words.

Part 1

Questions 1 – 7

There are 7 questions in this part.
For each question, there are 3 pictures and a short recording.
Choose the correct picture and put a tick (✔) in the box below it.

Example:

0 What time are they meeting?

A ☐   B ✔   C ☐

---

1 What didn't they see at the zoo?

 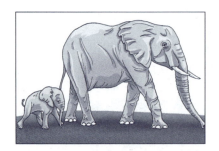 

A ☐   B ☐   C ☐

2 Which laptop did the woman buy?

A ☐   B ☐   C ☐

3 What is the man going to try?

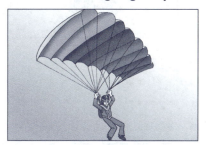  

A ☐ B ☐ C ☐

4 Which university is the man thinking of studying at?

A ☐ B ☐ C ☐

5 How will the application be sent?

A ☐ B ☐ C ☐

6 Who is the man's boss?

A ☐   B ☐   C ☐

7 Where are they going to go tonight?

A ☐   B ☐   C ☐

Hints on answering Listening, Part 2

Before you listen

Read the instructions so you know something about the text you will hear.

Quickly read each question stem (i.e., the first part of the sentence). If time allows, also read the choices. This will help you know what details to listen for: e.g., when, where, who, what.

As you listen

Look at your test booklet and listen for words in both the stem and choices. The speaker often mentions all 3 choices, but only 1 will correctly complete the statement or answer the question in the stem.

On the second listening, check your answers and answer anything you missed the first time.

Remember: Questions 8-13 are in the same order as the recording, but the answer choices may not be.

Part 2

Questions 8 – 13

You will hear a radio interview about keeping wild animals as pets.
For each question, put a tick (✔) in the correct box.

8	Dangerous Wild Animals Licences	**A**	are very surprising.	☐
		B	were popular between 1960 and 1970.	☐
		C	can be obtained from the Town Hall.	☐
9	Your application will take longer if you pay	**A**	150 pounds.	☐
		B	by credit card.	☐
		C	10% extra.	☐
10	The inspector will only give you a licence if you show that you intend to	**A**	treat the animal well.	☐
		B	tie the animal up.	☐
		C	keep the animal in a cage.	☐
11	You will not be given a licence if you	**A**	are under 18 years of age.	☐
		B	are planning to own an animal.	☐
		C	have had a licence in the past.	☐
12	The cheetah that Clive mentions	**A**	attacked its owner without any warning.	☐
		B	was sent to a wildlife park for about a year.	☐
		C	was given medical care for about a year.	☐
13	All licences are given	**A**	after regular inspections.	☐
		B	for a year at the most.	☐
		C	by animal welfare inspectors.	☐

Part 3

Questions 14 – 19

You are going to hear a vet talking about taking dogs on holiday.
For each question, fill in the missing information in the numbered space.

TAKING YOUR DOG ON HOLIDAY

Change of scene

Taking your dog on holiday is not that **(14)** …………….......................…… . Dogs like a change of scene as much as their owners do.

Cost

There are a lot of hotels where dogs can stay free of charge, although some do charge a **(15)** …………….........................…… .

Type of holiday

Choose your holiday with care. If you are going to be out a lot visiting **(16)** …………….........................…… , your dog might be happier in a kennel. If you want to take your dog sailing, go ashore often so the dog can get enough **(17)** …………….........................…… .

Things to take

Don't forget to take a water bowl, some dog food and your dog's favourite **(18)** …………….........................…… with you. You should also bring a blanket for the dog to sleep on and some rags to clean up muddy paw marks.

A final word of advice

If your holiday destination is far from home, take your dog on shorter **(19)** …………….........................…… journeys first, then gradually build up to longer and longer trips.

Part 4

Questions 20 – 25

Look at the 6 sentences for this part.
You will hear a conversation between a woman, Julie, and a man, Tom, about taking a year off before going to university.
Decide if each sentence is correct or incorrect.
If it is correct, put a tick (✔) in the box under **A** for **YES**. If it is not correct, put a tick (✔) in the box under **B** for **NO**.

		A YES	B NO
20	At first, Tom is surprised that Julie is taking a year off.	☐	☐
21	Julie thinks studying for exams is a waste of time.	☐	☐
22	Tom and Julie have the same opinion about working in an office.	☐	☐
23	Tom thinks Julie should work on a nature reserve.	☐	☐
24	Julie feels she should be paid more for her coaching job.	☐	☐
25	In the end, Tom supports Julie's decision.	☐	☐

Part 1 (2–3 minutes)

- Where do you live?

- Do you work or are you a student in ……..?

- Do you enjoy studying English? Why (not)?

- Do you think that English will be useful to you in the future?

- What do you enjoy doing in your free time?

Part 2 (2–3 minutes)

I'm going to describe a situation to you. You are planning to buy a pet for your younger brother. Talk together about different pets and decide which would be the best.

If you turn to page 148, you'll find some ideas to help you.

   [Pause for 4–5 seconds]

I'll say that again. You are planning to buy a pet for your younger brother. Talk together about different pets and decide which would be the best.

Part 3 (3 minutes)

Now, I'd like each of you to talk on your own about something. I'm going to give each of you a photograph showing students and teachers.

Candidate A, please look at photograph A on page 149.

Candidate B, you can also look at **Candidate A**'s photo, but I'll give you your photograph in a moment.

Candidate A, please tell us what you can see in your photograph?

   [Allow about 1 minute.]

Candidate B, please look at photograph B on page 149. It also shows students and teachers.

Candidate A, you can look also look at **Candidate B**'s photograph.

Now, **Candidate B**, please tell us what you can see in the photograph.

   [Allow about 1 minute.]

Part 4 (3 minutes)

Your photographs showed students and teachers. Now I'd like you to talk together about which lessons you find interesting and what teachers can do to make lessons more interesting.

Hints on handling the discussion in Speaking, Part 2

In this part of the test you are given a situation to discuss with your partner. For example, the task might be to talk about the different activities you can do at a place, and then decide on the best one based on some requirement or condition. The examiner will give you a picture sheet with ideas to help you. You and your partner will be given 2–3 minutes to speak together.

How to approach the task

You will find it much easier do this task if you treat the situation as a *real* situation.

For example:

- The task is to give advice on which of the items would be most useful to a friend who is going to study in England for 6 months.

- The picture sheet shows: a book, an umbrella, a dictionary, a map, a camera and a photograph of a family.

Think about someone you know well and consider how useful each of the items on the picture sheet would be to them.

When you are ready to begin, proceed as follows:

- Look at the picture sheet, and discuss the ideas one by one.

- Remember that part of your speaking mark is based on how you communicate with your partner. Whoever speaks first should give an opinion about one of the ideas or activities on the picture sheet. Then invite the other person to do the same. Use phrases like: 'What do you think?' or 'Do you agree?'

- The other person should comment *briefly* on the first idea/activity (e.g., 'I agree/disagree' or 'I think that's a good point') and then move on to comment on the next idea/activity.

- Continue taking turns until you cover all the ideas on the picture sheet, or until the examiner asks you to stop speaking.

Other helpful hints

- Be sure to include your partner in the conversation. If you speak too long or try to take over the conversation, you will lose marks.

- Try to support your opinions with examples and/or reasons.

- Remember that you don't have to agree with your partner. However, if you disagree, you should do so politely.

- Don't worry if you don't speak about all the ideas on the picture sheet. You are being marked on how well you speak and interact, not on whether or not you complete the task.

Reading

Questions 1 – 5

Look at the text in each question.
What does it say?
Mark the correct letter **A**, **B** or **C** on your answer sheet.

Example:

0

A Do not take photographs when speeding on this road.

B Cameras are used to check your speed on this road.

C You may use your high-speed camera on this road.

Answer:

1

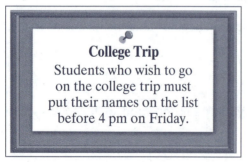

A The college trip will not take place if you don't sign up before Friday at 4 pm.

B If you would like to go on the trip, you must sign up before Friday at 4 pm.

C All students must sign the list to go on the college trip before Friday at 4 pm.

2

A Danny didn't remember to buy Laura's magazine.

B Laura is angry because Danny dropped her magazine.

C Laura would like Danny to collect her magazine for her.

3

A Phoning Customer Support costs the same as making a local call.

B Customer support is not available if you do not live in the area.

C You must call in at your local Customer Support Office for help.

4

TICKET OFFICE

Customers wishing to pay by credit card must present 2 pieces of identification.

A The theatre prefers customers to pay by credit card.

B You can't pay by credit card without proof of identity.

C You need proof of identity to apply for a credit card.

5

A Only emergency service vehicles can park here.

B You cannot park in this space if your car is dirty.

C You are only allowed to park here in an emergency.

Part 2

Questions 6 – 10

The people below are all looking for a TV programme to watch.
On the opposite page there are details of 8 programmes.
Decide which programme would be most suitable for the following people.
For questions **6 – 10**, mark the correct letter (**A – H**) on your answer sheet.

6  Arthur likes programmes about exploring space. He's a writer who likes to learn about astronauts, planets and the universe. Science-fiction films about extraterrestrials don't really interest him. ....

7  Georgia is a teacher who thinks some quiz shows are brilliant, but she's not keen on family quizzes or shows where the prize is money. Her favourites are the kind where the teams are people who work together. ....

8  Rick is a fireman. Because of his job, he works long hours and doesn't get to the shops too often. He loves watching shows where you can buy things. ....

9  Maria is a nurse who never seems to have any money to spend. She gets really excited when she sees people like herself win huge amounts of money, but she doesn't really like quiz shows. ....

10  Elaine has always wanted to be an astronaut. Her favourite TV shows are about astronauts in the future who meet people from other planets as they explore the universe. ....

This Week's Featured Programmes

A Travels in Space and Time
Here's another chance to see the award-winning documentary that originally aired as part of the Open University Science series. If you're studying science or you enjoy science documentaries, this is the show to watch!

B Make a Fortune
In this week's exciting contest, the Smiths from Wetherfield take on the Knowles from Granton. Which of the families will become the popular quiz show's next millionaires? Why not tune in and see for yourself?

C Sale of the Day
John Clyde shows us the latest 'must-have' technology and fashion items currently on the market. Don't forget to have your credit card ready. Phone lines will be open all night.

D Space Mission 3000
Captain Greg Davis and his extraterrestrial team continue their mission to find new planets. In this week's episode Zormborgs from the planet Zorm try to take over their spacecraft.

E May the Best Team Win
This week on the ever-popular general knowledge quiz, a team of lifeguards battles against a team of firefighters in an attempt to win the grand prize: an all-expenses-paid 2-week holiday in the USA!

F The Challenge
Excitement rises as 2 teams of health workers compete for the million-pound prize! This week's show includes a stretcher race and wheelchair basketball. Don't miss the fun!

G What, Why, How, Where, When?
If you've ever wondered how rockets fly or what the difference is between a galaxy and a solar system or a comet and a shooting star, this is the programme for you. This week's show includes an interview with NASA scientists who helped land a robot geologist on Mars.

H Shopper's World
In this week's special edition, the team takes you behind the scenes at your favourite Internet shopping sites. Take an inside look at problems like hidden costs and delivery charges, and prepare yourself for an inside report on the dangers of shopping online.

Part 3

Questions 11 – 20

Look at the sentences below about the Frequently Asked Questions on a website called SEA.
Read the text on the opposite page to decide if each sentence is correct or incorrect.
If it is correct, mark **A** on your answer sheet.
If it is not correct, mark **B** on your answer sheet.

		A	B
11	SEA is a website where you can sign up to learn about different sports.	▭	▭
12	The SEA website is only for professional athletes.	▭	▭
13	If you want to sell something on SEA, you must be a registered user.	▭	▭
14	Your auction can begin as soon as you click 'Place Item Up for Sale'.	▭	▭
15	If you want to buy an item, you don't have to pay the 'End Auction Now' price.	▭	▭
16	The most you can pay for an item is £10.	▭	▭
17	If you want to pay cash, you need to contact the seller.	▭	▭
18	People living outside the UK can also use the website.	▭	▭
19	If you buy something on the SEA website, you must collect it yourself.	▭	▭
20	If you change your mind about buying something, you must pay a small charge.	▭	▭

Hints on answering Reading, Part 3

In this part, you must decide whether 10 statements are true or false based on a long text. Here are some steps you may find helpful.

Look at each statement

- Read each statement carefully.
- Underline key words and phrases. This helps you to know what to look for in the text.

Find the information

- Look at the phrases you underlined and find the related information in the text.
- Remember that the statements are in the same order as the information in the text.
- If the text has headings, use them to help you. If it doesn't, you can usually tell what a paragraph is about by reading the first sentence.

Compare the statement with the text and then decide

- Carefully compare the statement with the related detail in the text.
- Remember that a statement will often use different words to express an idea in the text.
- Be careful when comparing sentences with quantity expressions or adverbs that have different meanings: for example, *few* vs. *some*; *not always* vs. *never*; *most of the time* vs. *sometimes*; *both … and* vs. *only*).

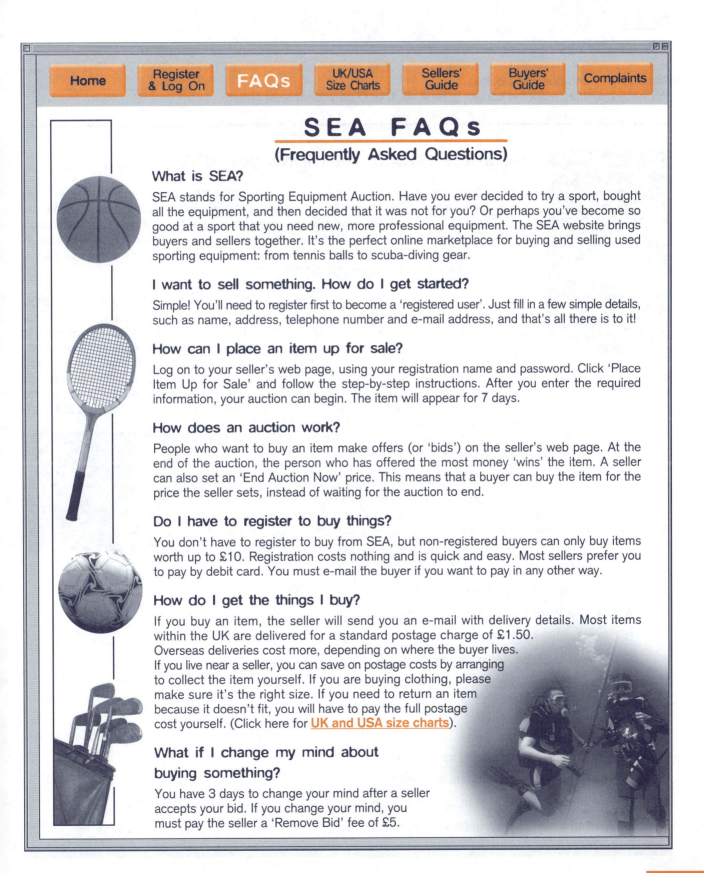

| Home | Register & Log On | FAQs | UK/USA Size Charts | Sellers' Guide | Buyers' Guide | Complaints |

SEA FAQs
(Frequently Asked Questions)

What is SEA?

SEA stands for Sporting Equipment Auction. Have you ever decided to try a sport, bought all the equipment, and then decided that it was not for you? Or perhaps you've become so good at a sport that you need new, more professional equipment. The SEA website brings buyers and sellers together. It's the perfect online marketplace for buying and selling used sporting equipment: from tennis balls to scuba-diving gear.

I want to sell something. How do I get started?

Simple! You'll need to register first to become a 'registered user'. Just fill in a few simple details, such as name, address, telephone number and e-mail address, and that's all there is to it!

How can I place an item up for sale?

Log on to your seller's web page, using your registration name and password. Click 'Place Item Up for Sale' and follow the step-by-step instructions. After you enter the required information, your auction can begin. The item will appear for 7 days.

How does an auction work?

People who want to buy an item make offers (or 'bids') on the seller's web page. At the end of the auction, the person who has offered the most money 'wins' the item. A seller can also set an 'End Auction Now' price. This means that a buyer can buy the item for the price the seller sets, instead of waiting for the auction to end.

Do I have to register to buy things?

You don't have to register to buy from SEA, but non-registered buyers can only buy items worth up to £10. Registration costs nothing and is quick and easy. Most sellers prefer you to pay by debit card. You must e-mail the buyer if you want to pay in any other way.

How do I get the things I buy?

If you buy an item, the seller will send you an e-mail with delivery details. Most items within the UK are delivered for a standard postage charge of £1.50. Overseas deliveries cost more, depending on where the buyer lives. If you live near a seller, you can save on postage costs by arranging to collect the item yourself. If you are buying clothing, please make sure it's the right size. If you need to return an item because it doesn't fit, you will have to pay the full postage cost yourself. (Click here for **UK and USA size charts**).

What if I change my mind about buying something?

You have 3 days to change your mind after a seller accepts your bid. If you change your mind, you must pay the seller a 'Remove Bid' fee of £5.

Part 4

Questions 21 – 25

Read the text and questions below.
For each question, mark the correct letter **A**, **B**, **C** or **D** on your answer sheet.

Roland Pearson, Astrophotographer

When I first started taking photographs of the night sky, I never thought I'd end up doing it for a living. I'd always been interested in photography. I used to drive my family and friends crazy because I was always taking photographs of them. Then one day I saw a poster of Earth taken from outer space. Posters like that were really popular in the 1970s. I had seen lots of them, but there was something different about this one. It fascinated me and it ended up changing my life!

It hasn't always been easy though. I remember trying to take a picture of the Hale Bopp Comet for a photography competition in 1997. I checked with experts at the local weather station to make sure they weren't expecting clouds or strong winds. At 3.30 am I set the camera up on a tripod in my garden, and then I began the countdown to 4 am, when the comet was scheduled to appear. I recall thinking, 'If everything goes as planned, the photo will show the comet as a line of light moving across a background of faint white stars.' But suddenly everything went terribly wrong! At 3.59, just as I was making the final adjustments, out of the bushes came a streak of black heading straight for my feet, and before I knew it the camera, tripod and I were on the ground! The streak of black was my neighbour's cat Tiddles out for his late-night exercise, and he had ruined the only chance I had for the next 2,000 years of capturing the spectacular comet on film!

But missed photo opportunities aside, astrophotography is a great job, and it can also be a fascinating hobby. Surprisingly enough, you don't need any special equipment: just a 35mm camera, a tripod and some slow-speed film. But you must remember to take care of your equipment. Otherwise that mysterious shadow on the moon's surface could be ruined by a tiny speck of dust on your camera lens!

21 In the text the writer describes

    A how he trained as an astrophotographer.

    B how he takes photographs for posters.

    C how he takes photographs of people.

    D how he became an astrophotographer.

22 What changed the writer's life?

    A taking family photographs for a living

    B taking up astrophotography as a hobby

    C becoming a popular photographer in the 1970s

    D seeing a poster of Earth taken from outer space

23 The writer's photograph of the Hale Bopp Comet was

  A meant for a competition.

  B ruined by a streak of light.

  C covered by a dark cloud.

  D taken just before 4 am.

24 The writer's photograph of the comet

  A turned out exactly as he had planned.

  B showed the comet moving across the sky.

  C was not taken because of a neighbour's cat.

  D could not be taken until the year 2000.

25 What might Roland say about his job?

  A
  > It's fascinating although it can be a challenge at times, and there are some unexpected problems.

  B
  > It's a really popular job, but you do have to spend a lot of time waiting.

  C
  > My photographs would be better if I had a lot more equipment.

  D
  > I drive my family and friends crazy because I'm always taking photographs.

Part 5

Questions 26 – 35

Read the text below and choose the correct word for each space.
For each question, mark the correct letter **A**, **B**, **C** or **D** on your answer sheet.

Example:

0	**A** at	**B** from	**C** to	**D** in

Answer:

0	A	B	C	D
	▭	▭	▬	▭

English Money

Before I came **(0)** .... England, I'd read about English customs. For example, I knew English people drove on the left side of the road. I knew that English people said 'please' and 'thank you' a lot and I knew **(26)** .... the money they used was called pounds and pence. It was quite a shock when I bought a newspaper and some mints at the airport, and the woman behind the counter said, 'That'll be 2 quid, love'. I made a quick calculation and decided to **(27)** .... over two £1 coins. Imagine my relief when she said 'Ta, love'. I didn't know what that **(28)** .... either, but at least she was smiling, so I must have got the money right.

I soon learned that a 'quid' is a pound. There are **(29)** .... explanations for this, but the one I like best is that 'quid' comes from 'Quidhampton Mill', which used to **(30)** .... the special paper that pound notes were printed on.

My new English friends often **(31)** .... about 'fivers' and 'tenners' but the meaning of these was obvious: a fiver is simply a £5 note and a tenner is a £10 note. They would **(32)** .... speak about things like computers or very old, used cars costing a 'grand' or a 'couple of grand'. It took me a while, but I finally figured out that a 'grand' was a thousand pounds.

Just when I thought I had **(33)** .... used to English money, I saw the following advertisement in a local newspaper: 'Wanted: Sales Clerk, London Area, £25k'. I was totally confused. I knew from my computer **(34)** .... that 'k' meant 'kilobyte'. I didn't **(35)** .... that it could also mean 'thousand' in newspaper advertisements. A few days later a friend explained the mystery. The advertisement was not for a 25-kilobyte clerk, but for a clerk who would earn £25,000 a year.

26	**A** why	**B** how	**C** that	**D** which

27	**A** go	**B** run	**C** do	**D** hand

28	**A** cost	**B** meant	**C** said	**D** did

29	**A** any	**B** couple	**C** little	**D** several

30	**A** grow	**B** produce	**C** build	**D** work

31	**A** talked	**B** discussed	**C** said	**D** told

32	**A** never	**B** also	**C** too	**D** ever

33	**A** done	**B** been	**C** got	**D** became

34	**A** course	**B** subject	**C** topic	**D** program

35	**A** feel	**B** say	**C** believe	**D** know

Writing

Part 1

Questions 1 – 5

Here are some sentences about shopping.
For each question, complete the second sentence so that it means the same as the first.
Use no more than 3 words.
Write only the missing words on your answer sheet.
You may use this page for any rough work.

Example:

0   Whose shop is this?

Who …………………………...…… **shop belong to?**

Answer:

0	does this

1   How much did your new jeans cost?

How much …….……………...………….. **for your new jeans?**

2   The jacket was so expensive that I didn't buy it.

It …….……………………………... **expensive jacket that I didn't buy it.**

3   Alan enjoys shopping for new clothes.

Alan …….……………………....…..…... **shop for new clothes.**

4   Shall I get you a larger size?

Would …….……………………………... **to get you a larger size?**

5   The shop had nothing on sale this week.

The shop didn't …….……..………………...……. **on sale this week.**

Part 2

Question 6

You have just heard about a new shop with some really good bargains.

Write a note to an English friend of yours. In your note, you should:

• say where the shop is.

• talk about what it sells.

• arrange to go there together.

Write **35 – 45 words** on your answer sheet.

Part 3

Write an answer to **one** of the questions (**7** or **8**) in this part.
Write your answer in about **100 words** on your answer sheet.
Put the question number in the box at the top of your answer sheet.

Question 7

- Your English teacher has asked you to write a story.

- Your story must begin with this sentence:

  I'd just taken the money to the police when I saw him.

- Write your **story** on your answer sheet.

Question 8

- This is part of a letter you receive from your English friend, Harry.

> I've just seen a programme about someone
> who won a million pounds. It was brilliant!
>
> What would you do if you won a lot of money?

- Now write a letter to Harry, answering his question.

- Write your **letter** on your answer sheet.

Using linking words and time expressions to improve your story

You can improve your story (and get a better mark) if you use linking words and time phrases to guide the reader through your story.

Here's an example without linking words or time expressions:

> *John and I had been walking down the street together. We saw a big envelope lying on the pavement. We didn't know what to do. John picked it up. He looked inside.*

Now look at how much better the story is when linking words and time expressions are added:

> ***Earlier that day*** *John and I had been walking down the street together **when** we saw a big envelope lying on the pavement. **At first** we didn't know what to do. **Then** John picked it up **and** looked inside.*

NOTE: For hints on using linking words in letters, see page 93.

Part 1

Questions 1 – 7

There are 7 questions in this part.
For each question, there are 3 pictures and a short recording.
Choose the correct picture and put a tick (✔) in the box below it.

Example:

0 What time are they meeting?

A ☐

B ✔

C ☐

---

1 How much did the woman pay for her new trainers?

A ☐

B ☐

C ☐

2 What is the woman going to wear to the football club party?

A ☐

B ☐

C ☐

3 Where did the man see the advertisement for a lifeguard?

A ☐

B ☐

C ☐

4 How will they pay for the coffee?

A ☐

B ☐

C ☐

5 What did the man write for his English class?

A ☐

B ☐

C ☐

6 Who rescued the man from the building?

A ☐   B ☐   C ☐

7 How did the man become a millionaire?

A ☐   B ☐   C ☐

Part 2

Questions 8 – 13

You will hear a man talking about problems with money.
For each question, put a tick (✔)in the correct box.

8   The speaker is going to talk about

    A   money as 'the root of all evil'.

    B   how the Bank of England prints money.

    C   forged and damaged bank notes.

9   What does the speaker ask the audience to do?

    A   give him some money

    B   look for a picture on a £5 note

    C   look at his collection of forged notes

10   A forged banknote will usually

    A   look extremely dirty.

    B   not have the words 'Bank of England'.

    C   feel completely smooth.

11   A £10 note is definitely a forgery if the broken metal line

    A   disappears when the note is held up to the light.

    B   appears broken when the note is held up to the light.

    C   appears solid when the note is held up to the light.

12   If you examine part of a £20 note with a magnifying glass, you will see

    A   the name of the Queen of England.

    B   the number '20' and the word 'twenty'.

    C   the word 'Queen' under a picture.

13   The most usual way in which banknotes are ruined is by being

    A   washed.

    B   heated.

    C   eaten.

Part 3

Questions 14 – 19

You will hear a woman talking about a training programme for firefighters.
For each question, fill in the missing information in the numbered space.

FIREFIGHTER TRAINING PROGRAMME

Duration
The course lasts for 3 months and includes training in how to use ladders, fire hoses and other
(14) …………….........................… equipment.

Programme
The goal of the course is to provide students with practice in putting out fires on trains, in
(15) …………….........................… and at petrol stations. The course helps students to become
accustomed to working in very hot, **(16)** …………….........................… places.

Who can apply
Applicants must be at least **(17)** …………….........................… of age and have a full driving licence.
You must also be very **(18)** …………….........................… and know how to be a good team member.

Remember: You will often be working when your friends are enjoying **(19)** …………….........................… .

Hints on answering Listening, Part 3

In this part you must fill in 6 gaps in a page of notes. The answers are usually numbers, single words (adjectives or nouns) or short noun phrases (1 – 2 words).

Before you listen
- Take notice of the headings in the test booklet. They will help you to focus on what to listen for.
- Read the notes quickly and ask yourself what's missing: a number? an adjective? a noun or noun phrase?

As you listen
- Look at each heading, and listen for the information that relates to it.
- Answer as many questions as you can the first time you listen.
- On the second listening, check the questions you already answered and fill in remaining gaps.

Remember:
- You will hear the words or phrases that you need in the recording. You will not need to change the form of any words.
- The questions follow the same order as the information you hear.

Part 4

Questions 20 – 25

Look at the 6 sentences for this part.
You will hear a conversation between a woman, Anna, and a man, Anthony, about shopping on the Internet.
Decide if each sentence is correct or incorrect.
If it is correct, put a tick (✔) in the box under **A** for **YES**. If it is not correct, put a tick (✔) in the box under **B** for **NO**.

		A YES	B NO
20	Anna thinks that the Internet is only good for buying electrical goods.	☐	☐
21	Anthony thinks Anna has a lot of clothes.	☐	☐
22	Anthony thinks order forms are difficult to fill in.	☐	☐
23	Anna would never order clothes over the phone.	☐	☐
24	Anthony doesn't like buying CDs online.	☐	☐
25	Anna is impressed by what Mark tells her.	☐	☐

Part 1 (2–3 minutes)

- Where do you live?

- Do you work or are you a student in ……..?

- Do you enjoy studying English? Why (not)?

- Do you think that English will be useful to you in the future?

- What do you enjoy doing in your free time?

Part 2 (2–3 minutes)

I'm going to describe a situation to you. Your best friend is moving to another town. You are thinking of giving him/her a present. Talk together about the presents you could buy for him/her, and decide which would be the best.

If you turn to on page 150, you'll find some ideas to help you.

[Pause for 4–5 seconds]

I'll say that again. Your best friend is moving to another town. You are thinking of giving him/her a present. Talk together about the presents you could buy for him/her, and decide which would be the best.

All right? Now talk together.

Part 3 (3 minutes)

Now I'd like each of you to talk on your own about something. I'm going to give each of you a photograph of workers who help to rescue people.

Candidate A, please look at photograph A on page 151.

Candidate B, you can also look at **Candidate A**'s photo, but I'll give you your photograph in a moment.

Candidate A, please tell us what you can see in your photograph?

[Allow about 1 minute.]

Candidate B, please look at photograph B on page 151. It also shows a worker helping to rescue someone.

Candidate A, you can look also look at **Candidate B**'s photograph.

Now, **Candidate B**, please tell us what you can see in the photograph.

[Allow about 1 minute.]

Part 4 (3 minutes)

Your photographs showed rescue workers and homes that people escaped from. Now I'd like you to talk together about what items you would take with you if you had to escape from your home and what items you would leave behind.

Hints on describing a photograph in Speaking, Part 3

In this part, you and your partner will each be asked to describe a photograph for 1 minute. That may not sound like a lot of time, but if you try it, you'll find that it's longer than you think! For that reason, it's important that you develop strategies to keep your description flowing.

Here are some helpful tips:

* Imagine you're talking to someone who can't see the photo. Give as many details as you can.

* Begin with an overall description. Use language like this:

    This is a photograph of a *man / woman / boy / girl* in a *shop / kitchen / office / restaurant*.
    The *shop / kitchen / office / restaurant* is very *nice / tidy / untidy / luxurious / big / small*.

* Then focus in on 1 or 2 of the people, and answer these questions:

What do they look like (e.g., height, weight, age, hair)?	How do you think they are feeling (e.g., happy, sad, excited, confused)?
What are they wearing?	Are there any other interesting objects/details?
What are they doing?	Where and when was the picture taken?

* Use **Present Simple** for permanent characteristics (e.g., It**'s** a photo of a family. / The man **has** short hair. / There **are** clouds in the sky.) and **Present Continuous** for things that are happening in the photo (e.g., She**'s wearing** a long red skirt. / They**'re sitting** on a bench in a park.)

* Remember to use linking words, and give as many details as you can.

Sample responses

Compare the following descriptions:

Candidate A: *This is a photograph of a man sitting at a table in a restaurant. The restaurant has a lot of plants. It looks nice. There aren't many people. The man is young. He is slim. He has got short fair hair. He is wearing a jacket and a shirt. I think he is a businessman. He is reading a newspaper. There are also some files, an organiser and a mobile phone. He is waiting for someone. He might be feeling hungry. The picture was taken indoors. The picture was taken in winter.*

Candidate B: *This is a photograph of a man sitting at a table in a restaurant. The restaurant has a lot of plants <u>and</u> looks very nice, <u>although</u> there aren't many people there at the moment. The man is young and slim <u>with</u> short fair hair. He's wearing a jacket and a shirt <u>so</u> I think he's a businessman. He's <u>also</u> reading a newspaper, <u>probably</u> the business page. There are also some things on the table <u>which</u> belong to the man: some files, an organiser and a mobile phone. <u>Perhaps</u> he's waiting for someone to arrive <u>so that</u> they can talk about business together. He might be feeling hungry <u>if</u> he's been waiting for a long time. This picture was taken indoors <u>and</u> I think it's winter <u>because</u> we can see his coat on the chair.*

Candidate A would not get a very high mark. Although the candidate makes no mistakes, he/she would have difficulty speaking for a full minute. Also, the sentences are quite simple and not well connected.

Candidate B would get a much higher mark. He/she has added ideas to the description and would have no difficulty speaking for the entire time. Note the variety of linking words that are used to combine details and ideas.

Reading

Questions 1 – 5

Look at the text in each question.
What does it say?
Mark the correct letter **A**, **B** or **C** on your answer sheet.

Example:

0

A Do not take photographs when speeding on this road.

B Cameras are used to check your speed on this road.

C You may use your high-speed camera on this road.

Answer:

1

A Airport employees must use this bus.

B All buses stopping here go to the airport.

C Some buses that stop here go to the airport.

2

A Only people looking for a job can go through this door.

B You can only go through this door if you own the company.

C Anyone who works for the company can go through this door.

3

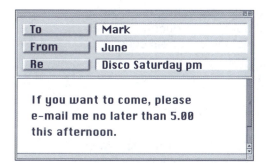

To	Mark
From	June
Re	Disco Saturday pm

If you want to come, please e-mail me no later than 5.00 this afternoon.

A Mark and June will be going to the disco together on Saturday afternoon.

B Mark should e-mail June before 5 pm if he wants to go to the disco on Saturday.

C June is worried that Mark might be late for their date at the disco on Saturday.

4

Free delivery
on items worth
£20 or more.

A Delivery is free if you spend at least £20.

B Delivery costs are usually more than £20.

C Delivery is not free if you spend over £20.

5

Use within 6 months of date printed on bottom of tin.

A The product must be used before the date printed on the tin.

B The product must be eaten within 6 months of purchase.

C The product should be used within 6 months of the date on the tin.

Part 2

Questions 6 – 10

The people below are all looking for voluntary work.
On the opposite page there are details of 8 charity organisations which are looking for volunteers.
Decide which organisation would be the most suitable for the following people.
For questions **6 – 10**, mark the correct letter (**A – H**) on your answer sheet.

6

Frank loves children, especially very young ones. He is training to be a nursery-school teacher during the week so he would only be able to volunteer at weekends.

....

7

Amy is a housewife with spare time on her hands. When she left school, she went to work in a clothing boutique, which she loved. Now that her children are at school, she wants to do some voluntary work during the week.

....

8

Lesley is a retired vet who would like to do voluntary work with animals. She often looks after her 3 grandchildren, so she would only be able to work for 1 or 2 days a week.

....

9

Sue has 3 small children. She's looking for a voluntary job she can do from home in the evenings, when her children are in bed. She's never worked, but her friends say she's a good listener and always gives them helpful advice.

....

10

After several years of studying, Lee has finally finished his degree in veterinary medicine. Before he finds a full-time job, he would like to take a year out to do voluntary work and travel abroad.

....

VOLUNTEERS NEEDED

A   Children in Need
We are looking for volunteers to help with a group of teenagers. If you are free on weekdays and would like to take a group of teenagers on visits to parks, museums and other places of interest, call us now on (01403) 230599.

B   Help the Children
This year we are going to have our first group of toddlers. If you enjoy being with pre-school children and don't mind giving up your Saturday mornings, apply now. Phone (01403) 777999 for details.

C   The Charity Shop
Do you have free time during the day? Would you like to help us by selling used clothes for various charities? If you are free for 5-6 hours on 1 or more weekdays, give us a ring on (01403) 531023.

D   Hobson Street School
We hold a jumble sale on the first Saturday of each month. Of course, your old clothes and other items are welcome, but if you'd like to help with the sale, please call our secretary on (01403) 899991.

E   Animal Shelter
Volunteers are needed to help take care of sick and injured animals. If you have some experience of working with animals and are free for a couple of days every week, call us now on (01403) 642135.

F   Tigers in Danger
Our organisation needs vets to help out in India. Volunteers will travel to nature reserves around the country. If you can work with us for 12 months, your return air fare will be paid. Phone (01403) 135531.

G   Help Line
Can you spend a few hours in the comfort of your own home, answering phone calls from people with problems? Day shift or evening shift available. Full training and special phone line provided free. Contact us on (01403) 846246.

H   Children's Home
We need people to help prepare evening meals for 50 young children. Volunteers will also be asked to help us clear up after the meal and supervise the children before they go to bed. Ring Mrs. Shaw on (01403) 957301.

Part 3

Questions 11 – 20

Look at the sentences below about a popular tour in England.
Read the text on the opposite page to decide if each sentence is correct or incorrect.
If it is correct, mark **A** on your answer sheet.
If it is not correct, mark **B** on your answer sheet.

		A	B
11	Tourists have been coming to Glastonbury for over 100 years.	▭	▭
12	King Arthur's Round Table can be seen at Glastonbury Abbey.	▭	▭
13	Joseph of Arimathea was born near Glastonbury Abbey.	▭	▭
14	Glastonbury Tor is an unusually shaped hill.	▭	▭
15	Stonehenge is not the biggest stone circle in the world	▭	▭
16	Avebury Henge is the most famous stone circle in Britain.	▭	▭
17	'The River Severn Tsunami' exhibition shows how the British countryside is changing	▭	▭
18	It is not clear how crop circles are formed.	▭	▭
19	You will have to pay extra for a room with a private bathroom.	▭	▭
20	The prices do not include a helicopter flight.	▭	▭

Avalon Tours

Glastonbury, the legendary Isle of Avalon, has been attracting visitors from all over the world for hundreds of years. It has long been at the centre of the legend of King Arthur and the Knights of the Round Table. In 1191, a cross with the words 'Here lies buried the renowned King Arthur in the Isle of Avalon' was found below Glastonbury Abbey.

Glastonbury Abbey is also well known as the birthplace of Christianity in Britain. Local legend says that Joseph of Arimathea founded the abbey, after burying the 'Chalice', or cup used by Jesus at the Last Supper, under nearby Chalice Well.

No visit to the area would be complete without visiting **Glastonbury Tor**, a strange, pyramid-shaped hill where you can see the remains of an ancient labyrinth. Images of the labyrinth can be seen on coins from ancient Crete, on columns at Pompeii and among the Hopi Indians of Arizona.

But perhaps the most famous place in this area is **Stonehenge**. Standing alone on Salisbury Plain,

Stonehenge is the best known of all stone circles. The history of Stonehenge remains a mystery, although some archaeologists think that the monument at Stonehenge may have been an ancient calendar. Also in this area is **Avebury Henge**, which although not as well known as Stonehenge, is the largest stone circle in the world.

You can also learn about a more recent event at 'The River Severn Tsunami' exhibition. The exhibition contains documents, drawings and other exhibits from 1607, when what is now thought to be a tsunami hit the River Severn, killing over 2,000 people and changing the surrounding countryside forever.

Even more recent is the appearance of strange patterns in fields, particularly in the Avebury area. Some people think that local people make these 'crop circles'; others believe that they are made by aliens. Whatever your opinion, when you see them, you'll have to admit that they are truly beautiful creations.

Choose from one of the following tours:

✦ KING ARTHUR'S AVALON
8 days, 7 nights
£ 995

✦ ISLE OF AVALON DELUXE
10 days, 9 nights
£ 1,295

All hotels used by Avalon Tours have a 4-star rating.
All rooms have private bathrooms and prices are based on 2 people sharing.
Some single rooms are available for a supplement of £180.
Helicopter flights available at an additional cost of £100.

Part 4

Questions 21 – 25

Read the text and questions below.
For each question, mark the correct letter **A**, **B**, **C** or **D** on your answer sheet.

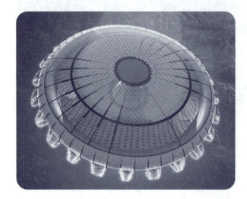

Veronica Jones, Flying Saucer Investigator

One evening about 20 years ago, I watched a documentary about how, in 1947, a 'flying saucer' had crashed in Roswell, New Mexico. Several people who had seen the crash were interviewed, including a nurse who said she had examined an alien who had been injured in the crash. At first, the people of Roswell were told that a flying saucer had crashed. Shortly afterwards they were told that it was not a flying saucer but a weather balloon. I decided that the only way I could learn the truth about flying saucers was to investigate them myself.

I have done a lot of research and although I still haven't discovered the truth about Roswell, I have discovered the truth about hundreds of other UFOs. A lot of UFOs are actually army planes or weather balloons, while others turn out to be natural phenomena like planets or comets. By far the largest number of UFOs turn out to be so-called 'fireball' meteors: slow-moving meteors that can take up to a minute to travel across the night sky.

When I'm investigating a UFO report, I arrange to meet the person at the place where they have seen the flying saucer. I like to interview a witness at the scene and then take photographs of the area. Then I speak to my contacts at local military bases and weather stations, and then check the witness's details against my information.

In about 95% of the cases I've dealt with, the 'flying saucers' turn out to be weather balloons, aeroplanes or natural phenomena. That still leaves 5% that, no matter what, just cannot be explained.

21 What is the writer's main purpose in writing the text?

   A to explain why she became a flying saucer investigator

   B to explain why she enjoys watching television documentaries

   C to describe how local weather stations use balloons

   D to describe how she discovered the truth about Roswell

22 Veronica says that UFOs

   A are always seen near weather balloons.

   B always travel across the sky slowly.

   C usually fly near natural phenomena.

   D often turn out to be a kind of meteor.

23 What will Veronica do if you think you have seen a flying saucer?

    A   meet you and ask you to describe what you saw

    B   take a photograph of you for her records

    C   ask you to take a photograph of it for her

    D   suggest that you contact a military base

24 When Veronica investigates a flying saucer, she

    A   makes sure that someone has taken of photo of it.

    B   always tells the local weather station before she arrives.

    C   can't find a logical explanation about 5% of the time.

    D   gives the witness the names of people who can help.

25 What would Veronica probably say about her job?

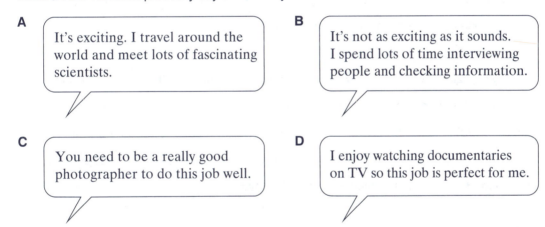

A It's exciting. I travel around the world and meet lots of fascinating scientists.

B It's not as exciting as it sounds. I spend lots of time interviewing people and checking information.

C You need to be a really good photographer to do this job well.

D I enjoy watching documentaries on TV so this job is perfect for me.

Hints on answering Reading, Part 4

Part 4 tests your ability to understand a writer's overall meaning, attitude and opinion. To do well, you need to leave enough time to read and think about the text very carefully.

Technique

- Look at the question stems before you read the text. This gives you an idea of what to look for.
- Read the first sentence of each paragraph to get a feel for the writer's purpose and overall meaning.
- As you do each question, think carefully about all 4 choices. Cross out those that are clearly wrong, then compare the ones that might be right. What proof can you find to help you decide?

Remember:

- Part 4 does not test factual information, so you probably won't find an answer in any single sentence. Instead, you'll need to read between the lines and consider several sentences or even paragraphs to answer most questions.
- You may find it easier to answer questions 21 and 25 last because they deal with the broader meaning of the text.
- The middle 3 questions follow the order of the text.

Part 5

Questions 26 – 35

Read the text below and choose the correct word for each space.
For each question, mark the correct letter **A**, **B**, **C** or **D** on your answer sheet.

Example:

0   **A**   deny   **B**   hope   **C**   believe   **D**   explain

Answer: | 0 | A   B   C   D |

Most people **(0)** ………. that fat is bad. If we get too fat, our **(26)** ………. don't fit properly and, more seriously, fat has been linked to all kinds of medical problems.

But fat is actually amazing. Thousands of years ago it was not always **(27)** ………. to find food, so **(28)** ………. peoples had to be able to eat plenty when food was available and to store excess food to keep them alive **(29)** ………. there was no food. There were no canned foods, no freezers, and **(30)** ………. of the techniques we use to store food nowadays. Miraculously, people's bodies turned excess food **(31)** ………. fat, which was stored in their cells!

But that's not all. Body fat also kept us warm when temperatures **(32)** ………. . Without body fat, we would never have **(33)** ………. the Ice Age.

So, the **(34)** ………. time you find yourself or a friend speaking negatively about fat, remember: If it wasn't for fat, we wouldn't **(35)** ………. here today!

26	**A**	dress	**B**	clothes	**C**	outfit	**D**	costume
27	**A**	hard	**B**	correct	**C**	difficult	**D**	easy
28	**A**	ancient	**B**	elderly	**C**	old-fashioned	**D**	older
29	**A**	as	**B**	until	**C**	after	**D**	when
30	**A**	some	**B**	all	**C**	none	**D**	any
31	**A**	from	**B**	up	**C**	into	**D**	on
32	**A**	dropped	**B**	fall	**C**	rose	**D**	increasing
33	**A**	existed	**B**	lived	**C**	continued	**D**	survived
34	**A**	last	**B**	next	**C**	every	**D**	second
35	**A**	have	**B**	be	**C**	work	**D**	stay

Writing

Questions 1 – 5

Here are some sentences about health.
For each question, complete the second sentence so that it means the same as the first.
Use no more than 3 words.
Write only the missing words on your answer sheet.
You may use this page for any rough work.

Example:

0   The nurse took her temperature.

She had ….…..............................…. **by the nurse.**

Answer:	0	her temperature taken

1   I don't get backache now that I've started exercising regularly.

I …..…...........................…... **backache before I started exercising regularly.**

2   Why don't you try to get more exercise?

If I were you, I ….…...........................…. **get more exercise.**

3   Listening to loud music caused his hearing problems.

His hearing problems …..….........................…… **listening to loud music.**

4   It's a long time since my dad has been to the doctor.

My dad ….…...........................…. **to the doctor for a long time.**

5   The patient did not recover from his illness for a long time.

The patient ….…...........................…. **a long time to recover from his illness.**

Part 2

Question 6

You are going to visit a haunted castle at the weekend.

Write a note to an English friend of yours. In your note you should:

• say which castle you are going to visit.

• mention who is organising the visit.

• invite your friend to go with you.

Write **35 – 45 words** on your answer sheet.

Part 3

Write an answer to **one** of the questions (**7** or **8**) in this part.
Write your answer in about **100 words** on your answer sheet.
Put the question number in the box at the top of your answer sheet.

Question 7

- This is part of a letter you receive from your English friend, Martha.

> I've just started a diet, and I've been going swimming every day. I think it's really important to stay fit. Do you agree?
>
> What do you do to keep fit?

- Now write a letter to Martha, answering her questions.

- Write your **letter** on your answer sheet.

Question 8

- Your English teacher has asked you to write a story.

- Your story must begin with this line:

    Last summer I saw the strangest sight I've ever seen.

- Write your **story** on your answer sheet.

Using linking words to improve your letter

You can improve your letter (and get a better mark) if you use linking words to join short sentences together.

The example below does not contain any linking words.

> *You asked me to write about my favourite restaurant. I will tell you about my favourite restaurant.*
> *My favourite restaurant is 'La Gondola'. I really like it. It's a very nice place. It has very good food.*
> *I usually go there at weekends. If there's a special occasion, I go during the week.*

Now look at how much better the letter is when linking words are added:

> *You asked me to write about my favourite restaurant,* **so** *let me tell you about it. My favourite restaurant is 'La Gondola'. I like it* **because** *it is a very nice place* **and** *it has very good food.*
> *I usually go there at weekends,* **but** *if there's a special occasion, I go during the week.*

When you read through your work again, always look for opportunities to join sentences in this way.

NOTE: For hints on using linking words and time expressions in stories, see page 71.

Part 1

Questions 1 – 7

There are 7 questions in this part.
For each question there are 3 pictures and a short recording.
Choose the correct picture and put a tick (✔) in the box below it.

Example:

0 What time are they meeting?

A ☐   B ✔   C ☐

---

1 What will the subject of next week's magazine article be?

   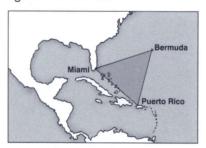   

A ☐   B ☐   C ☐

2 Which volunteer programme will the man join?

A ☐   B ☐   C ☐

3 What time is the man's appointment?

A ☐ B ☐ C ☐

4 What did the man want to be when he was younger?

A ☐ B ☐ C ☐

5 What made the woman feel uncomfortable?

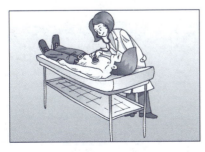 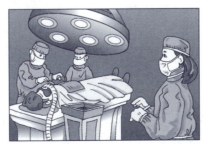 

A ☐ B ☐ C ☐

6 What was the previous week's story about?

A

B

C

7 What does the doctor give the woman?

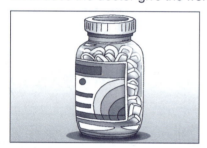

A

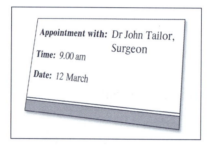

B

C

Part 2

Questions 8 – 13

You will hear a man called Jeremy being interviewed on the radio about his company, Made to Measure Mysteries. For each question, put a tick (✔) in the correct box.

8	Why did Jeremy and his friends arrange their first murder mystery party?	**A**	as a present for a friend's birthday	☐
		B	to start their business	☐
		C	to save money to go to Hollywood	☐
9	What gave Jeremy the idea for murder mystery parties?	**A**	mystery books written by a 62-year-old author	☐
		B	62 short stories he read when he was young	☐
		C	the mystery books he read when he was young	☐
10	Who usually attends Made to Measure Mystery parties?	**A**	university and college students	☐
		B	people of all ages	☐
		C	real detectives	☐
11	How many people are most of Jeremy's parties for?	**A**	a few dozen	☐
		B	several hundred	☐
		C	between 30 and 80	☐
12	Each time the company has a party they	**A**	try to get people to cooperate.	☐
		B	ask clients for ideas.	☐
		C	create a different script.	☐
13	Most of the company's parties	**A**	carry on for much more than 7 days.	☐
		B	are only for customers who are extremely rich.	☐
		C	are cheaper than taking friends out to eat.	☐

Part 3

Questions 14 – 19

You will hear a woman talking to a group of people during a very special visiting day at Fairfield Hospital. For each question, fill in the missing information in the numbered space.

FOUR-FOOTED FRIENDS VISITING DAY AT FAIRFIELD HOSPITAL

Background

Visits by dogs can make patients feel less alone and less frightened. It gives the patients something to **(14)** …………….........................… to.

Dogs make patients feel better. Even discouraged patients look happier when they see their dog **(15)** …………….........................… .

Training programme

Our visiting dogs are trained to become familiar with the unusual sights, sounds and **(16)** …………….........................… of hospitals.

They are also trained to **(17)** …………….........................… things for patients (such as toys, TV **(18)** …………….........................… , and cases for glasses).

Our dogs cannot visit a real hospital until they are taught these skills at our special college.

Use common sense

Volunteers should always make sure that their patients are not **(19)** …………….........................… to dogs.

Part 4

Questions 20 – 25

Look at the 6 sentences for this part.
You will hear a conversation between a man, Joe, and his friend, Debbie, about exercising.
Decide if each sentence is correct or incorrect.
If it is correct, put a tick (✔) in the box under **A** for **YES**. If it is not correct, put a tick (✔) in the box under **B** for **NO**.

		A YES	B NO
20	Joe isn't happy about his appearance.	☐	☐
21	Debbie agrees that Joe doesn't look good.	☐	☐
22	Joe thinks that going to a gym might be fun.	☐	☐
23	According to Debbie, going to a gym is not a waste of money.	☐	☐
24	Joe promises that he'll think about joining the gym.	☐	☐
25	Debbie is interested in starting an exercise routine with Joe.	☐	☐

Hints on answering Listening, Part 4

In this part you will hear a conversation between a man and a woman in which they express their attitudes and opinions about a certain topic. Your task is to decide whether 6 statements are true or false, according to what you hear.

Before you listen

- Be sure to read the second sentence of the instructions so you know (a) what the conversation is about and (b) what the names of the man and woman are.
- Read the 6 statements in your test booklet and underline the key information that comes after words/phrases like *thinks*, *believes*, *agrees*, *disagrees*, and *according to*. Also, be sure to circle negative words like *not*, *isn't*, *doesn't*, *won't*, and *never*. This helps you to know what to listen for.

As you listen

- Remember that the statements follow the order of what you hear.
- Look at each statement, and listen for information that relates to the words and phrases you've underlined and circled.
- Don't expect to hear the exact words in the statements. Remember that you are being tested on your ability to understand the overall meaning of what the speakers are saying.
- Answer as many questions as you can on the first listening.
- On the second listening, check your answers and fill in anything that you left blank on the first listening.
- If you're not sure, guess! You have a 50-50 chance of getting each question right.

Part 1 (2 – 3 minutes)

- Where do you live?

- Do you work or are you a student in …….. ?

- Do you enjoy studying English? Why (not)?

- Do you think that English will be useful to you in the future?

- What do you enjoy doing in your free time?

Part 2 (2 – 3 minutes)

I'm going to describe a situation to you. Your friend has asked you for advice on how to stay healthy. Talk together about different ways of staying healthy and decide which are the best.

If you turn to page 152, you'll find some ideas to help you.

   [Pause for 4-5 seconds]

I'll say that again. Your friend has asked you for advice on how to stay healthy. Talk together about different ways of staying healthy and decide which are the best.

All right? Now talk together.

Part 3 (3 minutes)

Now, I'd like each of you to talk on your own about something. I'm going to give each of you a photograph of people volunteering.

Candidate A, please look at photograph A on page 153.

Candidate B, you can also look at **Candidate A**'s photo, but I'll give you your photograph in a moment.

Candidate A, please tell us what you can see in your photograph?

   [Allow about 1 minute.]

Candidate B, please look at photograph B on page 153. It also shows people volunteering.

Candidate A, you can also look at **Candidate B**'s photograph.

Now, **Candidate B**, please tell us what you can see in the photograph.

   [Allow about 1 minute.]

Part 4 (3 minutes)

Your photographs showed people volunteering. Now I'd like you to talk together about the kinds of things you would volunteer for, and the kind of things you would *never* volunteer for.

Hints on handling the conversation in Speaking, Part 4

Part 4 is a conversation between you and your partner based on the theme of the photographs in Part 3.

It's important to remember that you are being marked on how you communicate and interact with your partner as well as how you express your ideas.

There are always 2 parts to this task. For example, the first part might ask about something positive ('Talk about voluntary work you would like to do'); and the second part might focus on something negative (e.g., 'Talk about voluntary work you would never do'). Other possibilities include 'then/now' tasks and 'specific/general' tasks: e.g., 'What were your preferences/experiences in the past?' and 'What are your preferences/experiences now?' or 'Talk about how you spend your free time' and 'Talk about how your friends spend their free time.'

How to approach the task

- Make sure you have understood *both* parts of the task. If you don't understand something or you haven't heard something clearly, don't be afraid to ask the examiner to repeat it.

- Deal with the first part first. Each of you should take a turn and then move on to the second part.

- If you speak first, you should give your ideas and then invite your partner to do the same. Use phrases like: 'What do you think?' 'Which do you prefer?' 'Do you agree?'

- If you go second, you must listen carefully to what your partner says and then respond to what he or she said. You can use language like: 'That's interesting' or 'I see' . When you finish, you might say something like, 'Should we move on to the other part now?' and then ask a question to help him or her get started: for example, 'So what kind of voluntary work would you *never* want to do?'

Other helpful hints

- Speak to your partner and *not* the examiner.

- Try to support your opinions with examples and/or reasons.

- Remember to show interest in what your partner is saying by nodding and making eye contact.

- If your partner gets stuck, you can help by suggesting a word or phrase to get him or her going again. But don't forget: Respect your partner's turn. If you speak too long or try to take over, you will lose marks.

- Remember that you don't always have to agree with your partner. If you choose to *disagree*, you should do so politely.

Reading

Part 1

Questions 1 – 5

Look at the text in each question.
What does it say?
Mark the correct letter **A**, **B** or **C** on your answer sheet.

Example:

0

A Do not take photographs when speeding on this road.

B Cameras are used to check your speed on this road.

C You may use your high-speed camera on this road.

Answer:

1

Crispy Cod

Place under a hot grill and cook for 20 minutes until crisp. Turn once.

A You must turn the Crispy Cod over after 20 minutes.

B The Crispy Cod will be ready in 20 minutes.

C You can eat the Crispy Cod with crisps.

2

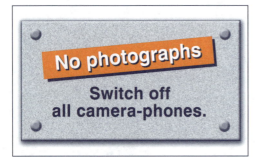

No photographs

Switch off all camera-phones.

A Camera-phones do not work in this area.

B You cannot buy photographs here.

C You must not take photographs here.

3

**NO DOGS
IN PLAYGROUND
UNLESS ON LEAD**

A You must keep your dog on a lead in the playground.

B Dogs on leads are not permitted in the playground.

C Your dog must walk behind you in the playground.

4

Hi, Karen,
Sorry, have to work tonight.
Maybe Rita can give you
a lift to party. If not, taxi
number is (856) 2317654.
                    Lenny

A Lenny doesn't want to work tonight.

B Lenny cannot take Karen to the party.

C Rita's phone number is 2317654.

5

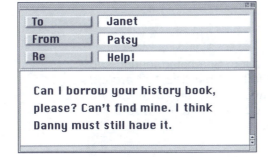

To	Janet
From	Patsy
Re	Help!

Can I borrow your history book, please? Can't find mine. I think Danny must still have it.

A Danny has borrowed Janet's history book.

B Janet wants to lend Patsy her history book.

C Patsy wants to borrow Janet's history book.

Part 2

Questions 6 – 10

The people below are all looking for jobs in advertising.
On the opposite page there are 8 job advertisements.
Decide which job would be suitable for the following people.
For questions **6 – 10**, mark the correct letter (**A – H**) on your answer sheet.

6

Maurice is 62 years old. He has been working as a photo model since he left school more than 40 years ago. For the past 10 years, he has specialised in modelling for travel magazines.

....

7

Lucy Dean is 25 years old with a degree in advertising. She writes clothing descriptions for a small but busy mail-order company. She doesn't mind the pressure, but she finds her job a bit dull and is looking for something more challenging.

....

8

Chang is in his late 40s and has been working for a large advertising agency for over 20 years. He's beginning to find it hard to cope with the long hours at the office, and he'd like a job where he doesn't spend so much time inside.

....

9

Sue is 20 and has just finished a graphics and photography course. She's an expert with digital cameras and has excellent computer skills. She wants a job where she can work on her own, as she's shy and doesn't like to deal directly with clients.

....

10

Alice used to be in a rock band. She hated touring and staying in hotels so she left the band to sail around the world with a friend and her family. She has no qualifications, so she is looking for a job where her music experience will be useful.

....

Opportunities in Advertising and Publicity

A A leading agency is looking for a trainee. All applicants must have completed a recognised photography course and be able to use a computer. The ideal candidate will be someone who doesn't mind working independently all day.

B Faces Modelling Agency is always looking for new talent. If you are between 16 and 21 and would like to be a model, fill in our application form now. Recent photo required. Remember: If you are under 18, please have your parents sign your application.

C The London Advertising Agency has a vacancy for a writer to take over from our present writer. This is a challenging job for someone who can work well in stressful situations. If you think you can create an image for anything from hairdryers to skateboards, call now for an application form.

D Are you tired of sitting behind a desk every day? Are you confident? Would you enjoy interviewing people in the street for a new consumer programme on TV? If your answer to these questions is 'Yes' and you have advertising experience, call us now for an application form.

E Trainee publicity agent required. The job includes booking hotel suites and arranging chat show appearances and celebrity autograph signings in department stores and record shops to advertise new films and albums. Our clients are famous actors and singers, and we even have a world-famous yachtswoman on our books.

F A leading magazine is looking for a staff writer for their new celebrity column. The job will include visiting film sets and attending award ceremonies. Applicants must be able to take shorthand and have word-processing skills. If you're interested, call us now to request an information package and application form.

G We are looking for a mature person to feature in our magazine advertisements for over-50s holidays. Candidates must have at least 10 years of modelling experience. Please send CV and examples of recent work with application.

H Buckstead Mail Order have a vacancy for a senior copy writer for their men and women's clothing department. The ideal candidate must have at least 15 years' experience writing mail-order copy and be willing to work long hours.

Part 3

Questions 11 – 20

Look at the sentences below about 2 different courses offered at a local university.
Read the text on the opposite page to decide if each sentence is correct or incorrect.
If it is correct, mark **A** on your answer sheet.
If it is not correct, mark **B** on your answer sheet.

		A	B
11	Anyone taking the Performing Arts course will attend a ceremony and be given a prize.	▭	▭
12	If you take the Performing Arts course, you will study 5 subjects.	▭	▭
13	All Performing Arts students will study costume and scenery design.	▭	▭
14	No qualifications are necessary to take the Performing Arts course.	▭	▭
15	Performing Arts students have classes every evening between 7 and 9 pm.	▭	▭
16	This is the first time the college is offering a Phobia Counselling course.	▭	▭
17	Before students sign up for Phobia Counselling, they must consult their family doctor.	▭	▭
18	Students must take part in the 'Fight That Phobia' campaign before they can become phobia counsellors.	▭	▭
19	An increasing number of people are afraid of discussing their phobias.	▭	▭
20	Part of the course is concerned with teaching people how to overcome their phobias.	▭	▭

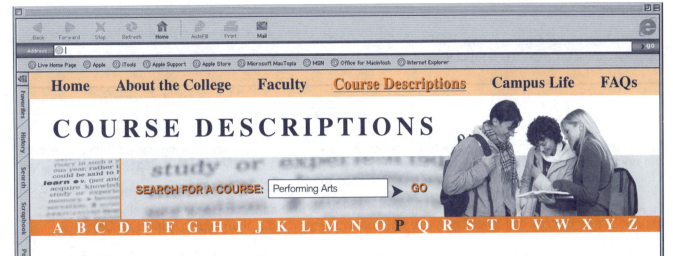

COURSE DESCRIPTIONS

Home   About the College   Faculty   **Course Descriptions**   Campus Life   FAQs

SEARCH FOR A COURSE: Performing Arts ▶ GO

A B C D E F G H I J K L M N O P Q R S T U V W X Y Z

Performing Arts

We can't guarantee you will be picking up an award at the next international film festival or that you will get the leading role in the next box-office hit; but we can guarantee that you will get the best possible training in the performing arts.

The course is 3 years long and is designed to improve your acting skills. Main subjects are Voice, Movement and Script Analysis. In addition, you will also be able to choose 2 subjects from the following: stage lighting, costume design, scenery design, theatrical production and theatrical writing.

During the course, you will develop qualities which will be useful to you in your career, such as communication and negotiating skills and the ability to meet deadlines under pressure.

This course has no formal entry requirements. Students must attend an audition. All students who pass the audition will be interviewed before they are offered a place on the course.

If you have acting talent and enjoy being the centre of attention, don't keep it to yourself. Come along to our open auditions any evening next week from 7 to 9 pm.

Psychology: Phobia Counselling

This year the Psychology Department will be offering a new course called 'Phobia Counselling'. We have introduced the course because of the increasing number of people consulting their family doctors about phobias. In the past, people have kept their phobias to themselves, but as a result of the recent 'Fight That Phobia' campaign, more and more people are admitting their fears.

The course is divided into 2 parts. Part 1 is the study of phobias, where we look at the theories of how these irrational fears develop and learn about all the different types of phobia. Part 2 is psychology-based and concentrates on ways of helping people to overcome their phobias using various methods, including new relaxation techniques and behavioural therapy.

Part 4

Questions 21 – 25

Read the text and questions below.
For each question, mark the correct letter **A**, **B**, **C** or **D** on your answer sheet.

Linda Johns, Hypnotist

When I first started working as a hypnotist, my friends thought it was a huge joke. Looking back, I can't blame them: the only hypnotists they had seen were the ones that get people to do silly things on stage, as part of a show. I have to admit that my parents weren't exactly thrilled by my choice of career either.

Everyone began to change their minds when I started work at the local hospital in the 'Stop Smoking' clinic. I suppose they thought that if doctors would consider working with me, then hypnosis must be OK.

I worked at the clinic for 3 years before setting up a phobia clinic in the centre of London. It came as a shock to realise just how many people have phobias that are ruining their lives.

I treat people of all ages and from all professions. Being in London, I am often consulted by celebrities – yes, they too have phobias. At first I felt very excited when I had a famous client. Over the years I've got used to seeing well-known faces in my office. Once they are away from the cameras, they are simply ordinary people – just like you and me.

21 What is the main purpose of this passage?

    A   to explain how Linda's family and friends gradually accepted her career

    B   to explain how her friends try to get tickets to see Linda's stage shows

    C   to describe how excited people were about Linda's choice of profession

    D   to describe the different stages of Linda's career as a professional hypnotist

22 What happened when Linda began working at the hospital?

    A   People began to take her profession more seriously.

    B   Some of the doctors didn't want to work with her.

    C   Her friends quit smoking after she hypnotised them.

    D   The doctors wanted to learn how to hypnotise people.

23   When Linda set up the phobia clinic, she

    A   was surprised at how many people have ruined their lives.

    B   began to realise how many people suffered from phobias.

    C   was only planning to work at the clinic for 3 years.

    D   was shocked when she realised how difficult the job was.

24   What does Linda say about celebrities?

    A   She has got to know them all very well.

    B   She gets very excited when they visit her.

    C   She treats many of them for phobias.

    D   A lot of them have phobias about cameras.

25   What would Linda say about her career?

    A
> I find it very satisfying when I am able to help people fight their fears.

    B
> I often regret not having a stage show and becoming a celebrity.

    C
> Although my career is a difficult one, it is often very amusing.

    D
> I get upset when medical professionals refuse to work with me.

Part 5

Questions 26 – 35

Read the text below and choose the correct word for each space.
For each question, mark the correct letter **A**, **B**, **C** or **D** on your answer sheet.

Example:

| 0 | **A** holiday | **B** occasion | **C** festival | **D** anniversary |

Answer:

| 0 | A ▭ B ▭ C ▭ D ▬ |

A Way with Words

It was my parents' wedding **(0)** ………. and I was looking for a card to buy them. I couldn't believe

(26) ………. awful the short verses on all the cards were. I remember thinking to **(27)** ………. ,

'Surely, **(28)** ………. can't all be that bad.' I was wrong. They were.

Even so, I never thought that one day I would be the person **(29)** ………. wrote them. I haven't

exactly made a **(30)** ………. , but I do **(31)** ………. a living by writing verses.

I can't think of a more perfect job. Every morning I wake up **(32)** ………. I like. I work from home,

so I don't have to drive to work every day. I don't have to take clients out for **(33)** ………. or try to

(34) ………. customers to buy anything. I just **(35)** ………. to sit at my computer, writing words that

will make people feel happy.

26	A	that	B	how	C	so	D	what
27	A	mine	B	me	C	my	D	myself
28	A	they	B	it	C	I	D	there
29	A	whom	B	which	C	who	D	whose
30	A	mess	B	fortune	C	place	D	mistake
31	A	gain	B	earn	C	win	D	take
32	A	however	B	whatever	C	whenever	D	wherever
33	A	meals	B	foods	C	dishes	D	plates
34	A	argue	B	make	C	use	D	persuade
35	A	used	B	want	C	ought	D	have

Hints on answering Reading, Part 5

In this part you have to fill 10 gaps in a text by selecting an answer from 4 options. Both vocabulary and grammar are being tested, so it's important to think about both as you do the exercise.

How to approach the task

*   Read the passage quickly without worrying about the missing words. This helps you to get a feel for what the passage is about before you start working.

*   Go back and work through each sentence. Think about what is missing: e.g., are you being tested on vocabulary, grammar, or maybe both?

*   Pay attention to the words before and after the gap, but also check the meaning of the whole sentence and the sentences around it. This is especially important when the choices are linking words, pronouns or verb forms.

*   Remember that the options for each question are always the same part of speech. Sometimes the words have similar meanings but they may be followed by different structures. For example:

    allow someone **to do** something   **make** someone **do** something
    let someone **do** something   **force** someone **to do** something

*   To check yourself, read the passage again. Ask questions like: 'Does my choice fit the meaning?', 'Are the linking words logical?', 'Are the pronouns, verb forms and other grammar features correct?'

*   Don't leave any answers blank. If you aren't sure, *guess*.

Writing

Part 1

Questions 1 – 5

Here are some sentences about celebrations.
For each question, complete the second sentence so that it means the same as the first.
Use no more than 3 words.
Write only the missing words on your answer sheet.
You may use this page for any rough work.

Example:

0   It took Sue a long time to decide what to wear for the party.

   Sue spent a long time ….....................................… **what to wear for the party.**

Answer: | 0 | *deciding* |

---

1   Do your parents let you stay up late on your birthday?

   Are you …....................................…….. **up late on your birthday?**

2   I've never seen such a big wedding cake.

   It's …......................................….. **cake I've ever seen.**

3   There weren't very many people at the party.

   There were only …......................................….. **people at the party.**

4   I would rather celebrate at a club than go to a restaurant.

   I like celebrating at clubs more than ….....................................….. **to restaurants.**

5   The manager advised us to book the hall early.

   The manager said ….....................................….. **book the hall early.**

Part 2

Question 6

You have lost your mobile phone at school.

Write a note for the school notice board. In your note you should:

• say when you lost your phone.

• describe your phone.

• tell people how to contact you if they find it.

Write **35 – 45** words on your answer sheet.

Part 3

Write an answer to **one** of the questions (**7** or **8**) in this part.
Write your answer in about **100 words** on your answer sheet.
Put the question number in the box at the top of your answer sheet.

Question 7

• Your English teacher has asked you to write a story.

• Your story must have the following title:

   The worst present I've ever received

• Write your **story** on your answer sheet.

Question 8

• This is part of a letter your receive from your American friend, Jill.

> Yesterday was Halloween. It was brilliant! Everyone was dressed up in amazing costumes, and we had a great time.
>
> What is your favourite celebration?

• Now write a letter to Jill, answering her question.

• Write your **letter** on your answer sheet.

Improving your stories with richer vocabulary

You can improve your story (and get a better mark) if you make an effort to use richer, more advanced vocabulary.

Look at this example:

> *My friends usually have **good** taste and buy me really **nice** gifts. But last year on my birthday I received a present that was really **bad**. I had **asked my friends to come** to a party at my house **on** my birthday. During the party they **gave** me the gift....*

Now look at how much better the story is when the simpler vocabulary words above are replaced with richer vocabulary:

> *My friends usually have **excellent** taste and buy me really **fantastic** gifts. But last year on my birthday I received a present that was really **awful**. I had **invited my friends** to a party at my house **to celebrate** my birthday. During the party they **presented** me with the gift....*

When you read through your work again, always look for opportunities to replace simple words with more advanced words that you know.

Part 1

Questions 1 – 7

There are 7 questions in this part.
For each question there are 3 pictures and a short recording.
Choose the correct picture and put a tick (✔) in the box below it.

Example:

0 What time are they meeting?

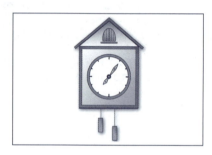

A ☐   B ✔   C ☐

---

1 When is Roy's birthday?

A ☐   B ☐   C ☐

2 Which activity is the woman *not* going to take part in?

A ☐   B ☐   C ☐

3 What is the man going to do on Thursday evening?

A

B

C

4 Which house belongs to the author?

A

B

C

5 What was the man in the advertisement advertising?

A

B

C

6 What time is the programme that the man would like to see?

A ☐   B ☐   C ☐

7 What will Mary take to the party?

A ☐   B ☐   C ☐

Part 2

Questions 8 – 13

You will hear an interview with a man who owns a company that organises party tours.
For each question, put a tick (✔) in the correct box.

8   What can you do on a Double the Fun bus?

    A   visit a university ☐

    B   take your friends on holiday ☐

    C   celebrate a special event ☐

9   What equipment do the buses have?

    A   somewhere to keep drinks cool ☐

    B   a place where people can dance ☐

    C   somewhere to cook food ☐

10   When guests go to a club, they

    A   must use a special entrance. ☐

    B   are always given a free drink. ☐

    C   must wait a while to be admitted. ☐

11   Where can a 3-course meal be served?

    A   in a client's own home ☐

    B   on the bus ☐

    C   in a restaurant ☐

12   Except in special cases, all guests must wear

    A   smart clothes. ☐

    B   jeans and trainers. ☐

    C   fancy-dress costumes. ☐

13   On a weekend away, tour guests

    A   will visit a museum. ☐

    B   can sleep on the bus. ☐

    C   will stay in a hotel. ☐

Part 3

Questions 14 – 19

You will hear a woman talking to a group of people about the Flying Phobia Clinic. For each question, fill in the missing information in the numbered space.

FLYING PHOBIA CLINIC
Notes on today's session

Introduction

- Thousands of people are affected by a phobia of flying.
- Flying is the **(14)** .... to travel. The chance of anything bad happening to you is about 1 in **(15)** ....
- The clinic guarantees that most of the group will totally overcome their phobia.

Morning session

- Talk at **(16)** .... by John Fleming about how planes fly.
- Question-and-answer session: box in **(17)** .... for members who are too embarrassed to ask questions.

Afternoon session

- 1.30   Sally Rodgers will show the group relaxation exercises in case anyone starts to **(18)** .... during the flight.
- 2.30   **(19)** .... flight

Part 4

Questions 20 – 25

Look at the 6 sentences for this part.
You will hear a conversation between a woman, Ruth, and a man, Gerry, about celebrities.
Decide if each sentence is correct or incorrect.
If it is correct, put a tick (✔) in the box under **A** for **YES**. If it is not correct, put a tick (✔) in the box under **B** for **NO**.

		A YES	B NO
20	Ruth doesn't think that celebrities are paid a lot of money.	☐	☐
21	Gerry thinks celebrities and athletes work long hours.	☐	☐
22	Ruth thinks celebrities should work in a factory or a hospital.	☐	☐
23	Gerry doesn't believe that celebrities have more money than they need.	☐	☐
24	Ruth agrees that celebrities have a difficult life.	☐	☐
25	Gerry thinks that some other professionals are paid too much money.	☐	☐

Part 1 (2 – 3 minutes)

- Where do you live?

- Do you work or are you a student in ....?

- Do you enjoy studying English? Why (not)?

- Do you think that English will be useful to you in the future?

- What do you enjoy doing in your free time?

Part 2 (2 – 3 minutes)

I'm going to describe a situation to you. You have been asked to make an advertising poster to attract more tourists to your country. Talk together about the pictures you could include, and decide which would be the best.

If you turn to page 154, you'll find some ideas to help you.

> [Pause for 4-5 seconds]

I'll say that again. You have been asked to make an advertising poster to attract more tourists to your country. Talk together about the pictures you could include, and decide which would be the best.

All right? Now talk together.

Part 3 (3 minutes)

Now, I'd like each of you to talk on your own about something. I'm going to give each of you a photograph showing different ways of spending free time.

Candidate A, please look at photograph A on page 155.

Candidate B, you can also look at **Candidate A**'s photo, but I'll give you your photograph in a moment.

Candidate A, please tell us what you can see in your photograph?

> [Allow about 1 minute.]

Candidate B, please look at photograph B on page 155. It also shows different ways of spending free time.

Candidate A, you can look also look at **Candidate B**'s photograph.

Now, **Candidate B**, please tell us what you can see in the photograph.

> [Allow about 1 minute.]

Part 4 (3 minutes)

Your photographs showed different ways of spending free time. Now I'd like you to talk together about how you spent your free time when you were younger and how you spend your free time now.

Do's and don'ts for improving your Speaking performance

Before you enter the Speaking test, it is a good idea to keep in mind the areas that the examiners will mark you on.

Here are some helpful **do's** and **don'ts** for the first 3 areas. (Tips for the last 2 areas are on page 145.)

	Do	**Don't**
Grammar and vocabulary	☺ Use grammar and vocabulary that you feel comfortable with. Your goal is to sound as natural and fluent as possible. ☺ Remember: This is not a vocabulary test.	☹ Experiment with expressions and idioms that you've just learnt. It's easy to lose marks by being too ambitious.
Discourse management (how well and appropriately you express yourself)	☺ Listen carefully so you can give appropriate answers. ☺ Ask the examiner or your partner to repeat anything that you haven't understood. ☺ Comment briefly on what your partner says, then give your own opinion. ☺ Support your ideas with reasons or examples.	☹ Ask the examiner to 'rephrase' a question. He or she is only allowed to repeat the question using the same words. ☹ Take over the conversation. You'll lose marks if you do.
Pronunciation (including stress, rhythm, intonation, sounds)	☺ Speak clearly and at a natural speed (neither too fast nor too slow). ☺ Try to keep your *ums* and *uhs* to a minimum.	☹ Put your head down or cover your mouth with your hand. This makes it hard for the others to hear what you're saying.

Reading

Part 1

Questions 1 – 5

Look at the text in each question.
What does it say?
Mark the correct letter **A**, **B** or **C** on your answer sheet.

Example:

0

A   Do not take photographs when speeding on this road.

B   Cameras are used to check your speed on this road.

C   You may use your high-speed camera on this road.

Answer: 0 | A B C

1

A   You get a free battery when you buy a packet of batteries.

B   If you buy only 1 packet, you do not have to pay for it.

C   If you buy 1 packet, you get a second packet without paying.

2

A   2-year-olds are too small to play this game.

B   2-year-olds should not play this game.

C   3-year-olds will enjoy playing this game.

3

A If Simon rents a DVD after 6 pm, he will have to pay extra.

B The video club closes at 6 pm, so Simon must not be late.

C If Simon returns the DVD before 6 pm, there is no late fee.

4

A Kelly has a dish that belongs to Wendy.

B Wendy wants Kelly to buy some fruit.

C Wendy borrowed a dish from Kelly.

5

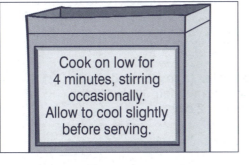

A This food will taste better if you eat it cold.

B This food must be stirred for 4 minutes.

C This food should not be served immediately.

Part 2

Questions 6 – 10

The people below are all looking for a new home.
On the opposite page there are 8 newspaper advertisements for houses and flats.
Decide which house or flat would be the most suitable for the following people.
For questions **6 – 10**, mark the correct letter (**A – H**) on your answer sheet.

6
Alan is a carpenter who has just retired. He is looking for a house with a lot of land around it. He doesn't mind having to do some repairs, but he doesn't like decorating.

....

7
Sean and Jenny are getting married next year. They plan to sell their flats and use the money to buy a new flat to live in after they marry. They prefer a place that is centrally located with lots of space.

....

8
Gill is moving back to Leeds after living in Germany for several years, so she wants to rent a furnished, well-equipped flat. She enjoys entertaining and expects lots of her German friends to visit.

....

9
Dan and Eva are in their mid-30s and are tired of living in flats. Eva just got a job in central Leeds, so they want to buy a small house close to her job. They love going out at night but hate having to drive home.

....

10
John and Sue have a daughter (aged 5) and a son (aged 7). They are looking for a modern house in the suburbs and need space for their 2 cars.

....

Flats and Houses Available:
Leeds and Surrounding Area

A Luxury flat to rent. Beautifully furnished. Huge dining area and large modern kitchen complete with brand-new refrigerator, cooker, and other electrical appliances. 2 bedrooms. Close to museums, concert hall, and shops.

B 4-bedroomed house, small garden, 30 minutes from centre. Needs a fair amount of work inside and out. Suitable for someone who's not afraid of doing a few repairs, putting up wallpaper and adding a fresh coat of paint.

C Bargain: large luxury flat near town centre. Relocating to Germany. Must sell within next 6 months. Cash buyers only.

D Large modern flat to let in quiet part of town out of the city centre. 1 bedroom. Ideal for young married couple.

E Brand-new 1-bedroomed house near children's playground. Short walk to local secondary school and sports facilities.

F 16th-century farmhouse, set in 2 acres of land. Very low price. Roof is damaged but inside is in excellent condition.

G New 3-bedroomed house near ring road. Double garage. Close to 2 primary schools and a secondary school.

H Small, 2-storey house for sale, central location, just 5 minutes' walk from pubs, clubs, restaurants and cinemas.

Part 3

Questions 11 – 20

Look at the sentences below about places to visit in Wales.
Read the text on the opposite page to decide if each sentence is correct or incorrect.
If it is correct, mark **A** on your answer sheet.
If it is not correct, mark **B** on your answer sheet.

		A	B
11	The advertisement features a famous hotel in Wales.	▭	▭
12	Conway Castle is the smallest castle in the world.	▭	▭
13	You don't have to travel by boat to get to the island of Anglesey.	▭	▭
14	The longest railway platform in the world is located in Anglesey.	▭	▭
15	It took the Welsh 700 years to finish building Beaumaris Castle.	▭	▭
16	Snowdonia is named after the highest mountain in Wales.	▭	▭
17	Betws-y-Coed is the name of a famous waterfall.	▭	▭
18	Clough Williams-Ellis bought the town of Portmeirion for under £5,000.	▭	▭
19	Wales has better weather than other parts of the British Isles.	▭	▭
20	You have to be at least 30 years old to do extreme sports in Wales.	▭	▭

Guide to pronouncing Welsh place names in the text

The Welsh language is extremely difficult to pronounce, unless of course you're Welsh! Here is a guide to help you with some of the trickier place names in the text:

Llanfairpwllgwyngythgogerychwyrndrobwllllantysiliogogogoch →
Thlan-vire [rhymes with 'fire']-poth-gwin-geth-go-gerick-wern-drobeth-thlanti-silly-o-gog-o-goch

Bettws-y-Coed   →   Bett-uh-see Koyd

Portmeirion   →   Port-merry-on

Beaumaris   →   Bow [rhymes with 'no']-mah-riss

Why go anywhere else?

Beaumaris Castle

Where can you visit ...

- 2 impressive castles
- the smallest house in the world
- a beautiful island
- a place with the longest name in Europe
- a waterfall
- an impressive mountain range
- an Italian square, complete with fountain

... and *still* be back at your hotel in time for dinner?

Give up? The answer is ... *Wales!*

Places of Interest

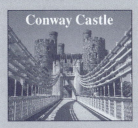

Conway Castle

Conway: On the North Wales coast, Conway is where you'll find the world's smallest house, as well as a much larger 'house', Conway Castle, which was built in the 13th century.

Anglesey: This beautiful island is joined to the rest of North Wales by a road bridge and a railway bridge, and it's just a short drive from Conway. Here you can visit the village of Llanfairpwllgwyngythgogerychwyrndrobwllllanty-siliogogogoch which, as any Welshman will tell you, means: 'Saint Mary's Church in the hollow of the white hazel near a rapid whirlpool and the Church of St. Tysilio of the red cave'. Don't miss the station:

the sign runs the complete length of the platform! Also on Anglesey is Beaumaris Castle, which was started in the 13th century and to this day remains unfinished.

Snowdonia: Just a couple of hours' drive from Beaumaris is the Snowdonia mountain range, which takes its name from the highest mountain in Wales, Mount Snowdon. From there, visit the famous Swallow Falls at nearby Betws-y-Coed.

Portmeirion: In 1925 Clough Williams-Ellis bought an attractive piece of Welsh land for less than £5,000. He then set out to show the world how a naturally beautiful site could be built on without being spoilt ... and spent the next 50 years building the Italian-style town of Portmeirion.

For more information, order our full-colour brochures:

- **Things to See in Wales**
  A more complete look at the full range of tourist attractions in this amazing part of the British Isles.

- **Wales: Sea, Sand and Sun**
  Wales has miles of beautiful coastline with long, sandy beaches plus 23 islands and more hours of sunshine each year than anywhere else in Britain. Get the inside story here.

- **Wales for the Fearless**
  Over 30 ideas for adventure activities and sports, both traditional and extreme.

Wales has it all!
Call (01234) 45632 to order brochures.

Part 4

Questions 21 – 25

Read the text and questions below.
For each question, mark the correct letter **A**, **B**, **C** or **D** on your answer sheet.

Garry Jones, Foley Artist

When I was about 8 years old, I decided I wanted to be a famous film star when I grew up. Well, I'm not a famous film star, but I do work for a film studio, and I do meet famous actors every day. I'm a Foley artist: I make the sounds that are added to films after they have been filmed.

Why does this need to be done? Well, if actors are filming a fight scene, you can't expect them to *really* hit each other or break each other's bones, so Foley artists have to find appropriate sounds. If you come into my studio and find me throwing wet towels at the walls and breaking carrots in half, don't worry. I'm just recording a fight scene.

When my kids were little, they loved our Christmas films because we always needed to record the sound of children walking on snow. It doesn't often snow in California so I had to create the sound in the studio. I used to cover part of the studio floor with salt crystals and pour a thick layer of flour over the top. Then I brought my kids and their friends to the studio so that I could record them walking in the 'snow'. After the recording, they never wanted to leave; they stayed and played, they got 'snow' in their shoes, on their clothes, even in their hair!

These days studios use computers to create such ordinary sounds as footsteps on snow. Some Foley artists see computers as a threat but I welcome the new technology. A lot of 'every day' sounds used to take a whole day to create, so there was a lot of pressure to get everything done on time. With computers, there's a lot less stress and I can devote more of my time to creating unusual sound effects. As long as people keep coming up with new ideas for films, studios will need Foley artists to come up with the sounds for them.

21   How does Garry Jones feel about his career?

    A   He's disappointed because he wants to be an actor.

    B   He feels happy because he often works with children.

    C   He's angry because computers will ruin his career.

    D   He enjoys it even more now than at the start.

22   Garry Jones

    A   imitates actors' voices.

    B   records sounds for films.

    C   helps injured actors.

    D   arranges fight scenes.

23 Why did Gary's children enjoy Christmas films?

    A   because they could play in the snow

    B   because they could earn extra money

    C   because they could play in the studio

    D   because they could visit California

24 Most modern studios

    A   spend a lot of money on computers.

    B   use a lot of ordinary sounds in films.

    C   use computers for everyday sounds.

    D   give Foley artists a lot of new ideas.

25 Which of the following is the best description of the writer?

    A

> **He is a man who enjoys his job and is positive about the future.**

    B

> **He is a man who enjoys spending free time with celebrities**

    C

> **He is a man who likes his job but wishes it was more creative.**

    D

> **He is a man who often uses new technology in his work.**

Part 5

Questions 26 – 35

Read the text below and choose the correct word for each space.
For each question, mark the correct letter **A**, **B**, **C** or **D** on your answer sheet.

Example:

| 0 | **A** wherever | **B** whichever | **C** whoever | **D** whatever |

Answer:

| 0 | A   B   C   D |

Blogs

A blog is your own web site. It's short for 'web log' and it's a place where you can write **(0)** ....
you want. It can be a chat site, a news page, a diary, a collection of articles or links to other sites:
all **(26)** .... a single page!

But it's not just a web site for people to read; it's interactive! People can read what you write and
make comments, **(27)** .... web links, chat, send you news, and so on. There are **(28)** ....
many possibilities!

There are millions of blogs by millions of people on millions of subjects. Your blog **(29)** .... be
anything you want it to be.

You could set **(30)** .... a blog about your **(31)** .... actor or singer. **(32)** .... you are
a part of a team or some kind of group, why not start a blog to **(33)** .... the group's news
and ideas?

Not sure how to **(34)** .... started? Try **(35)** .... out other peoples' blogs for interesting ideas.

26	**A** on	**B** of	**C** at	**D** to
27	**A** advise	**B** suggest	**C** tell	**D** look
28	**A** such	**B** not	**C** too	**D** so
29	**A** must	**B** would	**C** can	**D** will
30	**A** up	**B** out	**C** off	**D** down
31	**A** favourite	**B** best	**C** popular	**D** leading
32	**A** Because	**B** Whether	**C** As	**D** If
33	**A** divide	**B** deliver	**C** share	**D** split
34	**A** be	**B** get	**C** have	**D** become
35	**A** looking	**B** checking	**C** finding	**D** making

Writing

Part 1

Questions 1 – 5

Here are some questions about volunteering.
For each question, compete the second sentence so that it means the same as the first.
Use no more than 3 words.
Write only the missing words on your answer sheet.
You may use this page for any rough work.

Example:

0   If you want to volunteer, you can find information at your local library.

         If you are interested …..………………………….. , **you can find information at your local library.**

Answer:

0	in volunteering

1   It is not a good idea for Penny to volunteer as a lifeguard because she can't swim.

         Penny …..……………………........... **volunteer to be a lifeguard because she can't swim.**

2   The volunteers are raising money for the orphanage.

         Money for the orphanage …..…....…………………….. **raised by the volunteers.**

3   'Can you tell me where the Oxfam office is?' she asked me.

         She asked me …..…....…………………….. **her where the Oxfam office was.**

4   Susan has worked as a volunteer for several years.

         Susan …..……………………........... **work as a volunteer several years ago.**

5   I don't have enough free time to join a volunteer programme.

         I …..…....……………………….. **busy to join a volunteer programme.**

Part 2

Question 6

You are going to have a party at the weekend.

Write an e-mail to an English friend of yours. In your e-mail you should:

• say where and when the party is.

• explain why you are having the party.

• invite your friend to come to the party.

Write **35 – 45 words** on your answer sheet.

Part 3

Write an answer to **one** of the questions (**7** or **8**) in this part.
Write your answer in about **100 words** on your answer sheet.
Put the question number in the box at the top of your answer sheet.

Question 7

• This is part of a letter you receive from your English friend, Daniel.

> I've just got back from a new restaurant — it only opened tonight. The food was brilliant and there was great music.
>
> What's your favourite place to eat?

• Now write a letter to Daniel, telling him about your favourite place to eat.

• Write your **letter** on your answer sheet.

Question 8

• Your English teacher has asked you to write a story.

• Your story must begin with this sentence:

  When I opened my eyes, I realised it was only a dream.

• Write your **story** on your answer sheet.

Hints on organising your letter

Your letter will be better organised (and you will receive a higher mark) if you:

*   Start each paragraph with a **topic sentence** (a short sentence which tells the reader what the paragraph is about); and

*   Follow the topic sentence with 2 or 3 sentences which support the topic with examples or reasons.

Look at these paragraphs:

> La Bistro has dishes with meat, fish and chicken, as well as some very tasty vegetable dishes. The food is amazing. The desserts are absolutely fantastic. They are so big you can share them with a friend.

> You can go there with your friends because you will hear all the latest releases. You can also go to the restaurant with your parents because the music isn't too loud. The restaurant has great music.

Now look at how much better the paragraphs are when topic sentences are used:

> The food at La Bistro is amazing. There are dishes with meat, fish and chicken as well as some very tasty vegetable dishes. The desserts are absolutely fantastic. They are so big you can share them with a friend

> The restaurant has great music. You can go there with your friends because you will hear all the latest releases. You can also go with your parents because the music isn't too loud.

Try to use topic sentences in *all* your letters.

Part 1

Questions 1 – 7

There are 7 questions in this part.
For each question there are 3 pictures and a short recording.
Choose the correct picture and put a tick (✔) in the box below it.

Example:

0 What time are they meeting?

A ☐   B ✔   C ☐

---

1 Which number should you ring if you are calling from a phone in the Manchester area?

| 23633465 | 2363345 | 0161 2363345 |

A ☐   B ☐   C ☐

2 Where doesn't the man want to go again?

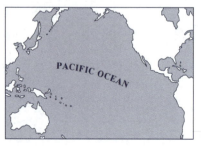

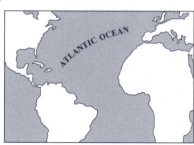

A ☐   B ☐   C ☐

3 Where did the woman leave her shopping list?

A ☐　　　　　　　B ☐　　　　　　　C ☐

4 Why doesn't the man want to visit the castle?

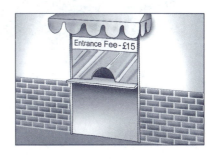

A ☐　　　　　　　B ☐　　　　　　　C ☐

5 What should the woman eat less of?

A ☐　　　　　　　B ☐　　　　　　　C ☐

6 What did the man forget to buy?

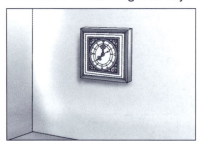

A   B   C

7 Where do the astronauts take the alien?

A   B   C

Part 2

Questions 8 – 13

You will hear a radio announcer talking about local exhibitions.
For each question, put a tick (✔) in the correct box.

8	What does the announcer say about *The Planets*?	**A**	It is on loan to the gallery.	☐
		B	It is his favourite painting.	☐
		C	It was done by a local artist.	☐
9	Which of the following is a sketch that is on display at the Whitford Gallery?	**A**	*The Sea*	☐
		B	*Holidaymakers*	☐
		C	*The Beach Party*	☐
10	What can you see if you go to the Grecian Gallery?	**A**	an exhibition about ancient museums	☐
		B	copies of ancient art	☐
		C	pottery made by local students	☐
11	If you want to enter the 'Clean Up Britain' competition, you must	**A**	travel to London.	☐
		B	take a photograph.	☐
		C	draw or paint a picture.	☐
12	What can you do at the Town Hall on Sunday morning?	**A**	arrange a birthday party	☐
		B	buy a gift for someone	☐
		C	celebrate a special occasion	☐
13	What does the announcer say about the exhibition at the Mansford Gallery?	**A**	It is cheaper than the other exhibitions.	☐
		B	It is open longer than the others.	☐
		C	Unlike the others, it is not free.	☐

Part 3

Questions 14 – 19

You will hear a woman talking to a group of people about a trip to France.
For each question, fill in the missing information in the numbered space.

TRIP TO FRANCE

Weather

- Cool during the evenings. Need sweater/sweatshirt.

- **(14)** ……………........……………………..… high during day. Bring suntan cream, sunglasses and swimming costume.

Rooms

- Toiletries like **(15)** …………….........………………………. provided.

- Hairdryer in every bathroom.

- Toothbrush and toothpaste: our own **(16)** …………………..........………………….....… .

The hotel

- **(17)** …………………........………………..… in every room.

- Cafeteria for snacks and drinks.

- **(18)** ……………….........………………..… on first floor.

- 2 pools: 1 indoor, 1 outdoor.

- Fully equipped **(19)** …………………........…………………….....… .

Reminder:

- Bring passport along.

Part 4

Questions 20 – 25

Look at the 6 sentences for this part.
You will hear a conversation between a woman, Alison, and a man, Justin, about books and computers.
Decide if each sentence is correct or incorrect.
If it is correct, put a tick (✔) in the box under **A** for **YES**. If it is not correct, put a tick (✔)in the box under **B** for **NO**.

		A YES	B NO
20	Justin thinks Alison's book is boring.	☐	☐
21	Alison doesn't like using her imagination.	☐	☐
22	There were some cartoons Justin disliked when he was younger.	☐	☐
23	According to Alison, Justin's computer is very valuable.	☐	☐
24	Justin agrees he spends too much money on his computer.	☐	☐
25	In the end, Alison feels that she can help Justin with his shopping.	☐	☐

Part 1 (2–3 minutes)

- Where do you live?

- Do you work or are you a student in ....?

- Do you enjoy studying English? Why (not)?

- Do you think that English will be useful to you in the future?

- What do you enjoy doing in your free time?

Part 2 (2–3 minutes)

I'm going to describe a situation to you. Your friend has asked you to help her to organise a party. Talk together about the different things you need for a party, and decide which are the most important.

If you turn to page 156, you'll find some ideas to help you.

    [Pause for 4-5 seconds]

I'll say that again. Your friend has asked you to help her to organise a party. Talk together about the different things you need for a party, and decide which are the most important.

Part 3 (3 minutes)

Now I'd like each of you to talk on your own about something. I'm going to give each of you a photograph showing people shopping for different things.

Candidate A, please look at photograph A on page 157.

Candidate B, you can also look at **Candidate A**'s photo, but I'll give you your photograph in a moment.

Candidate A, please tell us what you can see in your photograph?

    [Allow about 1 minute.]

Candidate B, please look at photograph B on page 157. It also shows people shopping for different things.

Candidate A, you can look also look at **Candidate B**'s photograph.

Now, **Candidate B**, please tell us what you can see in the photograph.

    [Allow about 1 minute.]

Part 4 (3 minutes)

Your photographs showed people shopping for different things. Now I'd like you to talk together about the kinds of things you enjoy shopping for and the kinds of things you dislike shopping for.

More do's and don'ts for improving your Speaking performance

Here are some helpful **do's** and **don'ts** for 2 more areas that you will be marked on. (Tips for the first 3 areas are on page 123).

	Do	**Don't**
Interactive communication	☺ Make eye contact. ☺ Show interest in what your partner says: nod your head and use language like *Good idea*! and *Yes, I agree*. ☺ Invite your partner to comment with phrases like *Do you agree?* or *What do you think*? ☺ Try to help if your partner gets stuck.	☹ Speak in your native language. ☹ Take over the conversation. ☹ Stop speaking for so long that the flow of communication breaks down.
Overall performance	☺ Remember to say 'please' and 'thank you'. ☺ Be yourself. It's easier to relax if you don't try to impress the examiners with ideas you think they want to hear. ☺ Complete each task to the best of your ability with well-supported ideas. ☺ Keep the conversation going, and remember to always involve your partner.	☹ Prepare a speech for Part 1. If you do, the examiner will not let you finish. ☹ Describe the drawings in Part 2. They are there only to give you ideas about the topic. ☹ Panic if you can't think of a specific word when discussing the photo in Part 3 and the theme in Part 4. Use other words to say what a thing is used for or what a person does. ☹ Worry if you make a few mistakes. The examiners are more interested in your ability to communicate.

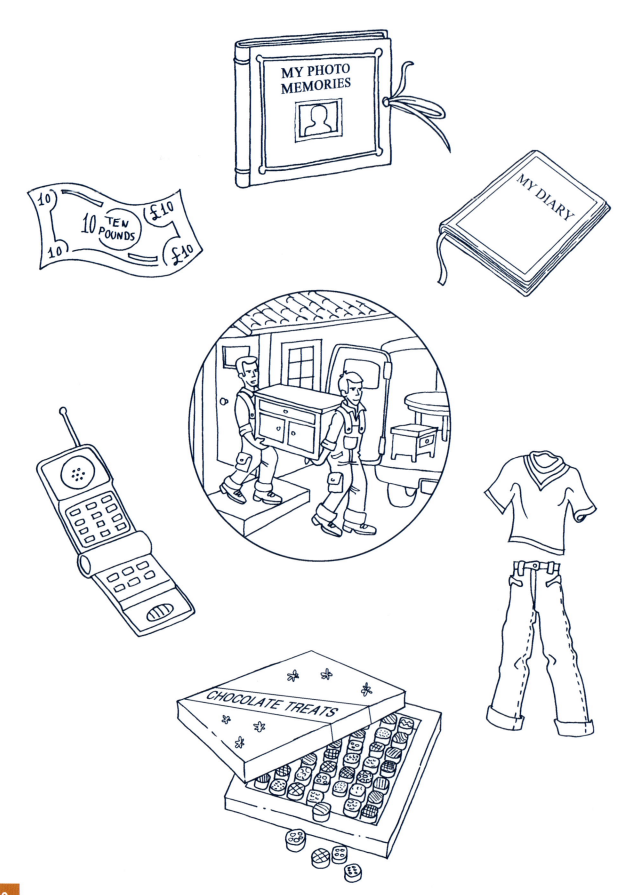

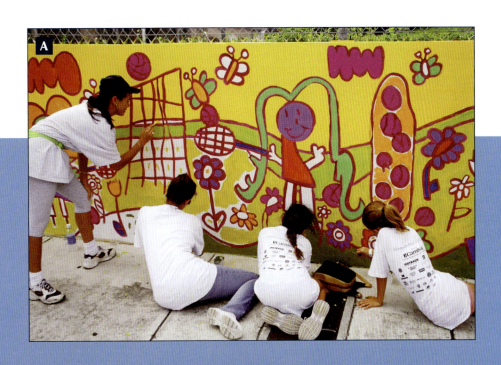

Study the vocabulary used in **Test One**, and then try the exercises below.

A   SIMILAR BUT DIFFERENT - Use the words in the box to fill the gaps in each group.

1   **famous   popular**

a   Mini-skirts are back in style. After the 1960s, I never thought they'd be .... again.

b   The actor is very .... , but not many people like him.

2   **fun   funny**

a   It was .... to go dancing with you. Let's do it again some time.

b   Mike tells such .... jokes. He always makes me laugh!

c   Thanks for a lovely time. I really had ....

3   **true   honest**

a   She likes reading books based on .... stories.

b   Brenda is very .... She always tells the truth.

4   **some   any   no**

a   Are there .... eggs in the fridge? I want to make an omelette.

b   There are .... eggs in the fridge. I can make an omelette.

c   There are .... eggs in the fridge. I used them all to make an omelette.

5   **interested   interesting**

a   Mark is very .... in subjects like maths and physics.

b   I read a really .... book last week.

B   QUESTIONS WITH *LIKE* - Draw a line between each matching question and answer.

1   What is Julie like?

2   What does Julie like?

3   What does Julie look like?

a   She likes going to the cinema and playing volleyball.

b   She's tall and slim, with long curly black hair.

c   She's really friendly. Everyone likes her.

C   ADVERBS - Use one of the words in the box to fill the gap in each sentence.

enough   quite   so   too   very

1   He is .... tired to come to the party.

2   The runner was .... fast that he finished the marathon an hour before the others.

3   You say you waited for him for 90 minutes? That's a .... long time!

4   My 10-year-old brother isn't old .... to drive a car.

5   I .... like strawberry ice cream, but chocolate is my favourite.

Study the vocabulary used in **Test Two**, and then try the exercises below.

A SIMILAR BUT DIFFERENT - Use the words in the box to fill the gaps in each group.

1 | measure | count |

  a We'd better .... the fridge to see if it will fit in the kitchen.

  b Did you .... your money to see if you have enough to get on the bus?

2 | hear | listen |

  a Didn't you .... the telephone ring?

  b .... carefully. I'm going to give you some very important information.

3 | hard | hardly |

  a Colin studied really .... for the test; I'm sure he'll do well.

  b Mary .... studied for the test; I don't think she will pass.

4 | while | since | unless |

  a .... Sue was finishing her homework, Mike was upstairs listening to CDs.

  b She's lived in London .... she was 6 years old.

  c .... you study, you won't pass the test. The teacher says it will be difficult.

5 | under | down |

  a Will you please get .... ? You might fall and hurt yourself.

  b The boat sailed .... the bridge.

B COMMON EXPRESSIONS - Use the words in the box to fill the gaps in the sentences.

| believe | catch | dying | earn | put |

1 Mark wants to be a doctor. How do you want to .... a living when you are older?

2 Alan knew the answer so he tried to .... his teacher's eye.

3 Mike has just passed his driving test and is .... to take his friends for a ride.

4 When Sally left university, she couldn't wait to .... her new skills to the test.

5 .... it or not , my grandmother has just learned to windsurf.

C ADJECTIVES - Use the words in the box to complete the gaps in the paragraph.

| favourite | funny | local | perfect | safe | wild |

I work at the **(1)** .... zoo. It's a great occupation. In my job I look after a lot of
(2) .... animals. My parents thought it was really dangerous at first, but now they know it's
absolutely **(3)** .... My **(4)** .... animals are the chimpanzees. They always make
me laugh because they do such **(5)** .... things. I love what I do and I'm really happy in my work.
I believe I have found the **(6)** .... job for me.

Study the vocabulary used in **Test Three**, and then try the exercises below.

A SIMILAR BUT DIFFERENT - Use the words in the box to fill the gaps in each group.

1 | subject | lesson |

   a   My favourite .... at school was geography.

   b   I have an English .... every Monday, Wednesday and Friday morning.

2 | talk | discuss |

   a   The teacher said we mustn't .... during the test.

   b   The politicians are meeting tomorrow to .... the economic crisis.

3 | say | tell |

   a   I won't give you the ice cream if you don't .... 'please'.

   b   The teacher is going to .... us our marks on Friday.

4 | believe | know |

   a   I don't .... in ghosts.

   b   I don't .... if he's telling the truth or not.

5 | see | watch |

   a   I read in a magazine that cats can .... in the dark.

   b   I don't usually .... the news on TV. I prefer to read a newspaper.

B *TAKE* - Match the bold phrases on the left with their meanings on the right.

1 .... Will the aliens **take over** the planet?   **a** start (something new)

2 .... The meeting will **take place** at 10 am this Wednesday.   **b** gain control of

3 .... Did the couple **take up** any hobbies when they retired?   **c** look after

4 .... Our team will **take on** last year's champions next week.   **d** happen

5 .... Maria is old enough to **take care of** her younger sister.   **e** compete against, challenge

C PREPOSITIONS - Use the words in the box to fill the gaps in the sentences.

| in | out | up |

1 I never thought Ben would end .... working as a teacher. He always hated school!

2 We didn't expect things to turn .... the way they did.

3 Remember to tune .... to see who wins tonight's mystery prize.

4 Nancy has signed .... for a cookery class at the local evening centre.

5 Why don't you call .... on your way home from work.

6 I wish I could figure .... the solution to the problem

Study the vocabulary used in **Test Four**, and then try the exercises below.

A   **SIMILAR BUT DIFFERENT - Use the words in the box to fill the gaps in each group.**

1   **outfit   costume**

   a   Tanya needs to buy a new .... to wear for job interviews.

   b   Sam wore a wizard's .... to the party. He looked just like Harry Potter.

2   **ancient   elderly   older**

   a   Len has 2 .... sisters: Beverly, who is 14; and Kate, who is 16.

   b   Our next-door neighbour is a lovely .... woman in her mid-80s.

   c   There are many .... buildings in Greece. The most famous is the Parthenon.

3   **advice   advise**

   a   I asked the careers officer to give me some .... about a career in banking.

   b   Bank managers can .... people on how to invest their money.

   c   I never ask my parents for .... I prefer to ask my friends.

4   **exist   live   survive**

   a   Computers did not .... in the 16th century.

   b   It is feared that some of the passengers did not .... the crash.

   c   I hope I never have to .... through such a terrible experience.

B   **COMMON EXPRESSIONS - Use the words in the box to fill the gaps in the sentences.**

have time on their hands	**remain a mystery**	**take a year out**	**work full time**

a   They'd like to volunteer more, but they .... and can only help out at weekends.

b   When they retire, they'll .... Perhaps they'll volunteer at the orphanage.

c   The origins of the crop circles in this area ....

d   Mike and Fran are planning to .... and do some travelling before they look for permanent jobs.

C   **LINKING WORDS – Use the words in the box to fill the gaps in the sentences.**

as	**until**	**then**	**when**

1   I went to the supermarket .... I wanted to buy some food.

2   I put a loaf of bread, a dozen eggs and a carton of milk in my basket, and .... I went to the checkout.

3   I waited in the queue for 20 minutes .... I finally got to the front.

4   I was just about to pay the cashier .... I realised I had left my money at home.

Study the vocabulary used in **Test Five**, and then try the exercises below.

A SIMILAR BUT DIFFERENT - Use the words in the box to fill the gaps in each group.

1 | **meal** | **food**

   a   We'll have to order a pizza; there's no .... in the house.

   b   We had an excellent .... at the Chinese restaurant last night.

   c   Which kind of .... do you prefer – French, Chinese or Indian?

2 | **borrow** | **lend**

   a   Wayne asked if he could .... £50 until next week.

   b   Wayne asked me if I could .... him £50 until next week.

3 | **argue** | **persuade**

   a   Pete and Jenny never agree. They always find something to .... about.

   b   I tried to .... my boss to give me more money, but she refused.

4 | **talent** | **skill**

   a   Kate has a real .... for art. She's never had lessons, but she can draw anything.

   b   Like arithmetic, reading is a basic .... that is taught in primary school.

5 | **whenever** | **wherever** | **whatever**

   a   When Mary is home, her little sister follows her around .... she goes.

   b   I'll be home all day so come over .... you can.

   c   He says he will do .... he can to help us.

B COMMON EXPRESSIONS - Use the words in the box to fill the gaps in the sentences.

complete   **fill**   **give**   **make**   **meet**

1   The teacher said he would .... a prize for the best composition.

2   It's easy to open a bank account. All you have to do is .... in a form.

3   'If you don't .... the deadline, you'll be fired,' the manager said angrily.

4   I didn't realise you were still at university. When do you expect to .... the course?

5   Tom's business is really doing well. If it keeps up like this, he'll .... a fortune!

C PREPOSITIONS - Use the words in the box to fill the gaps in the sentences.

about   **in**   **into**   **on**   **with**

1   The teacher showed the children how to divide small numbers .... big numbers.

2   Frank hopes to specialise .... ancient history at university.

3   I don't know how students cope .... all the homework they have to do.

4   Please turn the music down; I can't concentrate .... my book.

5   Last week we read an interesting article .... Asia.

Study the vocabulary used in **Test Six**, and then try the exercises below.

A SIMILAR BUT DIFFERENT - Use the words in the box to fill the gaps in each group.

1 | **suggest**   **advise**

   a If you're looking for a good book, I'm sure the librarian can .... something.

   b I .... you to think carefully before you quit your job.

2 | **divide**   **share**

   a If you .... 9 by 3, the answer will be 3.

   b Their new house has 4 bedrooms so Ed doesn't have to .... a room with his sister.

3 | **facilities**   **equipment**

   a Our town has excellent sports .... , including a gym, an indoor swimming pool and a football pitch.

   b You can buy tennis racquets and other sports .... at the sports shop in the High Street.

4 | **normal**   **usual**

   a Liam's temperature was above .... so his mother called the doctor.

   b As .... , the teacher started the lesson right on time.

5 | **coat**   **layer**

   a When they woke up, there was a thick .... of snow on the ground.

   b The sitting room would look better with a fresh .... of paint.

B PHRASAL VERBS WITH *UP* - Match the bold phrases on the left with their meanings on the right.

1	.... Most young children can't wait to **grow up**.	a	stop trying
2	.... Don't **give up**! I'm sure you can find the answer.	b	make (something) ready to use
3	.... I find it really hard to **get up** sometimes.	c	become an adult
4	.... Did you **sign up** for the pottery class?	d	get out of bed
5	.... How long will it take to **set up** the equipment?	e	think of, invent
6	.... I wonder what excuse he'll **come up with** this time!	f	put your name on a list

C PREPOSITIONS - Complete the gaps in the paragraph with *for* or *from*.

When I was looking **(1)** .... a job, I saw an ad **(2)** .... a magician's assistant. I thought it would be fun, so I answered the ad. It took a while to hear **(3)** .... him, but the magician, the Incredible Marvo, finally called! He told me I would be well paid **(4)** .... my work, so I took the job. We did shows at a number of theatres in the area and sometimes I didn't get back **(5)** .... work until after midnight. When it was time to pay me, he said he couldn't because he hadn't received any money **(6)** .... the theatres yet. To make matters worse, he asked if he could borrow money **(7)** .... me **(8)** .... the taxi home!

PAPER 1: Reading and Writing - Candidate answer sheet 1

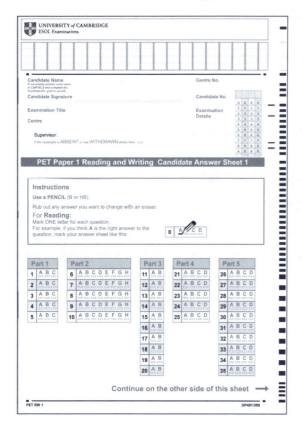

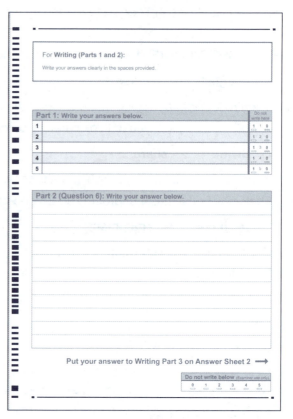

PAPER 1: Reading and Writing - Candidate answer sheet 2

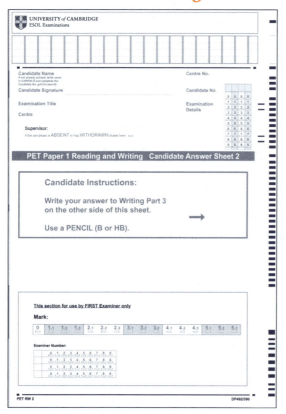

PAPER 2: Listening - Candidate answer sheet

UNIVERSITY of CAMBRIDGE
ESOL Examinations

Candidate Name
If not already printed, write name
in CAPITALS and complete the
Candidate No. grid (in pencil).

Candidate Signature

Examination Title

Centre

Supervisor:
If the candidate is ABSENT or has WITHDRAWN shade here ▭

Centre No.

Candidate No.

Examination Details

PET Paper 2 Listening Candidate Answer Sheet

You must transfer all your answers from the Listening Question Paper to this answer sheet.

Instructions

Use a PENCIL (B or HB).

Rub out any answer you want to change with an eraser.

For **Parts 1, 2** and **4:**
Mark ONE letter for each question.
For example, if you think **A** is the right answer to the
question, mark your answer sheet like this:

| 0 | A̶ | C |

For **Part 3:**
Write your answers clearly in the spaces next
to the numbers (14 to 19) like this:

| 0 | example̶ |

Part 1	Part 2	Part 3	Do not write here	Part 4
1 A B C	8 A B C	14	1 14 0	20 A B
2 A B C	9 A B C	15	1 15 0	21 A B
3 A B C	10 A B C	16	1 16 0	22 A B
4 A B C	11 A B C	17	1 17 0	23 A B
5 A B C	12 A B C	18	1 18 0	24 A B
6 A B C	13 A B C	19	1 19 0	25 A B
7 A B C				

PET L

DP493/391

CENGAGE
Learning·

Cambridge PET Practice Tests
Dorothy Adams with Diane Flanel Piniaris

Acknowledgments

The publishers would like to thank Visual Hellas for permission to reproduce copyright photographs.

PET answer sheets reprinted with the permission of University of Cambridge ESOL Examinations, Cambridge, England.

Illustrations by Theofanis Skafidas

Recording at GFS-PRO Studio by George Flamouridis

© 2006, Cengage Learning EMEA

For product information and technology assistance, contact **emea.info@cengage.com**. For permission to use material from this text or product, and for permission queries, email **emea.permissions@cengage.com**.

British Library Cataloguing-in-Publication Data
A catalogue record for this book is available from the British Library.

ISBN: 978-960-403-329-4

Cengage Learning EMEA
Cheriton House, North Way, Andover, Hampshire, SP10 5BE
United Kingdom

Cengage Learning products are represented in Canada by Nelson Education, Ltd.

For your lifelong learning solutions, visit **www.cengage.co.uk**

Purchase your next print book, e-book or e-chapter at **www.cengagebrain.com**

Printed in Greece by Bakis
6 7 8 9 10 – 17 16 15 14 13